DOGFIGHT 9

F4F Wildcat
South Pacific 1942–43

Edward M. Young

OSPREY PUBLISHING
Bloomsbury Publishing Plc
Kemp House, Chawley Park, Cumnor Hill, Oxford,
OX2 9PH, UK
29 Earlsfort Terrace, Dublin 2, Ireland
1385 Broadway, 5th Floor, New York, NY 10018, USA
E-mail; info@ospreypublishing.com
www.ospreypublishing.com

OSPREY is a trademark of Osprey Publishing Ltd

First published in Great Britain in 2023

© Osprey Publishing Ltd, 2023

A catalogue record for this book is available from the British
Library.

ISBN: PB 9781472854865; eBook 9781472854834;
ePDF 9781472854841; XML 9781472854858

23 24 25 26 27 10 9 8 7 6 5 4 3 2 1

Edited by Tony Holmes
Cover and battlescene artwork by Gareth Hector
Ribbon and tactical diagrams by Tim Brown
Armament artworks by Jim Laurier
Maps by www.bounford.com
Index by Alison Worthington
Typeset by PDQ Digital Media Solutions, UK
Printed and bound in India by Replika Press Private Ltd.

Osprey Publishing supports the Woodland Trust, the UK's
leading woodland conservation charity.

To find out more about our authors and books visit
www.ospreypublishing.com. Here you will find extracts, author
interviews, details of forthcoming events, and the option to sign
up for our newsletter.

Front Cover Artwork: On August 24, 1942, during the first day
of the Battle of the Eastern Solomons, Machinist Donald
Runyon of VF-6 was leading a division of F4F-4 Wildcats from
USS *Enterprise* (CV-6) when he was directed to intercept a
formation of Type 99 Carrier Bombers from *Zuikaku* heading for
his carrier and USS *Saratoga* (CV-3). Diving from out of the sun
at 20,000ft, Runyon flamed one "Val" before pulling up for
another high-side pass. He then "flamed" a second "Val." As
Runyon was climbing up to make a third pass on the bombers,
a Zero-sen (which Runyon described as a "Nagoya Zero") from
Zuikaku attacked him from above and behind. Its pilot made the
fatal mistake of pulling out his diving pass below and ahead of
Runyon's Wildcat, allowing him to open fire at close range. The
Zero-sen exploded.

Runyon then resumed his attack on the carrier bombers,
"flaming" a third to take his tally to four Japanese aircraft shot
down in just a matter of minutes. Of the nine Type 99 Carrier
Bombers in the formation, intercepting Wildcats from *Saratoga*'s
VF-5 and *Enterprise*'s VF-6 shot down seven – two more were
forced to ditch on their return flight. During August 1942
Runyon claimed eight Japanese aircraft shot down, becoming the
US Navy's leading ace in the F4F Wildcat. (Cover artwork by
Gareth Hector)

Previous Page: The pilots of VMF-112 pose in front of an F4F-4
with the squadron scoreboard, which shows 74 victories, at
Henderson Field in early June 1943. The unit was in the process
of converting to the F4U-1 Corsair when this photograph was
taken. (Tony Holmes Collection)

Acknowledgments – I would like to express my gratitude to the
late Frank Olynyk, who over many years compiled extensive lists of
US Navy and US Marine Corps aerial victory claims during World
War II. In preparing the background to the F4F Wildcat's service
in the South Pacific, I found John Lundstrom's works on US Navy
fighter units in the first year of the war invaluable (Selected
Sources). I would like to thank the Museum of Flight in Seattle,
Washington, for permission to quote from interviews with Donald
L. Balch, Leonard K. Davis, William B. Freeman and Michael R.
Yunck, all part of The American Fighter Aces Association Oral
Interviews collection. These are available digitally at the Museum's
website: https://digitalcollections.museumofflight.org/collections/
show/280. I have also used an excerpt from *Aces Against Japan –
The American Aces Speak Volume 1* by Eric Hammel, with the
permission of Presidio Press, an imprint of Random House, a
division of Penguin Random House LLC.

I would also like to thank Nicole Davis at the Museum of Flight
for permission to use photographs from the Albert J. Bibee and the
John W. Lambert collections. Thank you also to the staff of the
Still Pictures Branch at Archives II, National Archives and Records
Administration, College Park, Maryland, for their exceptional
service, and to fellow Osprey author and leading Southwest Pacific
War historian Michael Claringbould for information on A6M
Zero-sen and Ki-43-I "Oscar" colors and markings. Finally, I
would like to express my appreciation to Tim Brown, Gareth
Hector, and Jim Laurier for their wonderful artwork.

DOGFIGHT

Contents

CHAPTER 1
IN BATTLE

Shortly after dawn on August 7, 1942, 16 F4F-4 Wildcats of VF-71 took off from USS *Wasp* (CV-7), part of Task Force (TF) 61, to strike the Imperial Japanese Naval Air Force (IJNAF) seaplane base near the island of Tulagi, directly north of Guadalcanal. Joining the fighters were 15 SBD Dauntless dive-bombers from VS-71, and nine more from VS-5 embarked in USS *Enterprise* (CV-6). F4Fs and SBDs also took off from *Enterprise* and USS *Saratoga* (CV-3) to support the US Marine Corps landing on Guadalcanal.

Lt Cdr Courtney Shands, VF-71's CO, led 11 Wildcats around the northern end of Tulagi, which was nestled in an inlet next to the appreciably larger Florida Island, looking for four-engined H6K Type 97 flying boats (soon to be christened "Mavis" under the Allied system of assigning simple names to Japanese aircraft). Three of the aircraft from the Yokohama Kokutai were moored at two small islets to the east of Tulagi. Shands and his division quickly found them off Makambo Island, and all three flying boats were destroyed, along with several auxiliary vessels servicing them.

Following the destruction of the H6K, the F4F division flew east until six A6M2-N Type 2 Floatplane fighters ("Rufes") were spotted and then strafed. All of them were set on fire.

To the south of the island, Lt S. Downs Wright and Ens Roland Kenton flew around the southern tip of Tulagi toward Gavutu and Tanambogo islets, where they found a further four moored Type 97s and destroyed all of them. Both Naval Aviators then shot up several other objects on the water which they thought were also flying boats. As Downs Wright noted in his Aircraft Action Report, his first attack on the Type 97s was from east to west as dawn broke:

> Fired on first 97 at extreme range, starting a fire, continued down and straight over first boat toward two more. Short bursts set both of these on fire. Climbing turn over hills of island and back down to set two more 97s on fire. Noted two others burning.

Downs Wright and Kenton then strafed the buildings and docks on Gavutu, while Shands and his pilots attacked installations at Halavo harbor on nearby Florida Island. SBDs bombed the harbor once the F4Fs had completed their strafing runs.

Alerted to the American attacks on Tulagi and the landings at Guadalcanal, the 5th Koku Kushu Butai (5th Air Attack Force) on Rabaul immediately prepared a response, sending out 22 G4M Type 1 Land-Based Attack Bombers ("Bettys") from 4th Kokutai. They were escorted by 17 A6M2 Zero-sen fighters from the Tainan Kokutai on the long 560-mile flight to Guadalcanal. Nine D3A Type 99 Carrier Bombers ("Vals") from 2nd Kokutai were also sortied.

Approaching Guadalcanal through cloud cover, the bombers descended beneath the overcast to release their ordnance on the US Navy vessels offshore. Two divisions of VF-5 Wildcats on a combat air patrol (CAP) found the bombers and went in to attack them, only to be bounced by five Tainan Zero-sens and have three F4Fs shot down. Ens Donald Innis and Lt Herbert Brown claimed two Zero-sens damaged in the attack, while Lt James Southerland and Ens Joseph Daly claimed two bombers apiece. Shortly after

F4F-4 Wildcats from VF-71 prepare to take off from *Wasp* on August 7, 1942 to support the US Marine Corps landings on Guadalcanal. Earlier that day, the squadron had attacked the Japanese seaplane base near the island of Tulagi, destroying seven H6K flying boats and eight A6M2-N floatplane fighters. (80G-14054, RG 80, NARA)

Machinist Donald Runyon of VF-6, embarked in *Enterprise*, claimed two D3A Type 99 Carrier Bombers shot down on August 7 and a G4M Type 1 Land-Based Attack Bomber and a Zero-sen on August 8. He was subsequently credited with three more D3As and a Zero-sen during the Battle of the Eastern Solomons on August 24. (80G-14205, RG80, NARA)

hitting the bombers, Daly also came under attack from a Zero-sen and bailed out when his Wildcat burst into flames. Southerland, too, was shot down, parachuting to safety. In the space of a few minutes VF-5 had lost five (of eight) Wildcats to the A6M2s.

Following VF-5's attack on the bombers, ten Wildcats from VF-6 chased the "Bettys" as they withdrew in the direction of Rabaul. Lt(jg) Theodore Gay Jr's division attacked the bombers, claiming one confirmed, two probables, and two damaged, although one of the escorting Zero-sens hit Machinist Julius Achten's Wildcat badly enough that he had to ditch his damaged fighter near an American transport vessel.

Shortly thereafter, Lt(jg) Gordon Firebaugh led his five Wildcats in to attack the bombers. He ordered two of his pilots to engage the "Bettys" while his section took on the fighter escorts. Firebaugh appeared to hit a Zero-sen, only to be bounced by two more fighters that hit his Wildcat and shot down his wingman, AP1c William Stephenson. Nevertheless, Firebaugh continued to fire at the Zero-sens as they "flashed" past, claiming two shot down before his F4F was repeatedly hit and set on fire. It was at this point that Firebaugh bailed out. Other members of Firebaugh's division claimed two bombers and a Zero-sen destroyed.

Later that afternoon, the nine ill-fated Type 99 Carrier Bombers ran into VF-5 and VF-6, losing five shot down – the remaining four aircraft had to ditch near the Shortland Islands when they ran out of fuel. VF-5 and VF-6 pilots were credited with 14 Type 99s shot down, with several making multiple claims.

The next day, August 8, the 5th Koku Kushu Butai sent out a large force of G4M Type 1 Land-Based Attack Bombers armed with torpedoes, with a Zero-sen escort, to attack the US Navy carriers now known to be operating off the Solomons. When search aircraft failed to find the vessels, the "Bettys" instead targeted transports off Guadalcanal in low-level torpedo attacks. Anti-aircraft fire from the assembled ships claimed eight bombers shot down.

Flying above at 17,000ft, Machinist Donald Runyon was leading two other Wildcats patrolling over the American ships. Hearing of the torpedo attack, he led the fighters down and saw five "Bettys" retiring after completing their runs. Runyon missed his target on his first attack, but Ens Will Rouse set another bomber on fire. Runyon then made a head-on attack against a bomber and shot it down. Rouse went after a third G4M and set it on fire, although he was in turn bounced by a Zero-sen. Breaking off his attack on the smoking "Betty," Rouse fled in the direction of Runyon, who duly shot down the pursuing

Zero-sen in a head-on attack. Ens Joe Shoemaker, the third member of Runyon's division, claimed a fourth "Betty" destroyed.

Concerned about the possibility of more attacks from Japanese land-based aircraft, Vice Adm Frank Fletcher, commanding TF 61, decided to withdraw his carriers to the south. In the fiercely contested combats of August 7, TF 61's three fighter squadrons (VF-5, VF-6, and VF-71) had lost 15 Wildcats from the 99 available. Tainan Kokutai Zero-sens had downed nine F4F, with the remaining six destroyed in operational crashes or through battle damage. In the conclusions of a report on the air actions of August 7–8, the *Enterprise* carrier air group listed the challenges facing US Navy and US Marine Corps Wildcat pilots in the South Pacific in the coming year of aerial combat:

1. The F4F-4, considering equality of pilots, is no match for the Japanese Zero fighter in a dogfight, plane for plane, due to superiority of the Zero in climb, speed, maneuverability, and endurance. However, in its ruggedness, ability to "take it," and firepower, the F4F-4 is superior to the Zero. These factors of priority, combined with an apparent superiority of our pilots in deflection shooting, give the F4F-4 a reasonable chance of attaining a successful outcome in an engagement in which there are several fighters involved on both sides. The principal weaknesses of the Zero are (1) inability to absorb hits, and (2) ineffective firepower.

2. It is now believed that the best defense for the F4F-4 against Zero attack is for each plane of the two-plane element to turn away and then turn immediately toward each other and set up a continuous "scissors" [the defensive maneuver Lt Cdr John "Jimmy" Thach had recently developed]. Thus, when a Zero bears

Maj John L. Smith was the leading US Marine Corps ace of the early fighting on Guadalcanal. He led VMF-223 onto the island on August 20, 1942, and in nearly two months of intense combat claimed 19 Japanese aircraft shot down, including eight Zero-sens. (Tony Holmes Collection)

in on one of the F4Fs, the other F4F is in a position to fire on the Zero. A short, accurate burst from the F4F is generally sufficient to knock down the Zero, whereas the F4F can absorb almost unbelievable punishment from the Zero.

Shortly thereafter, US Marine Corps Wildcat pilots would confront the Zero-sen for the first time in the Solomons when Capt John L. Smith (soon to be promoted to Major) led VMF-223, equipped with 19 F4F-4s, into the recently named Henderson Field on Guadalcanal on August 20. The unit would share the airfield with 12 SBDs from VMSB-232.

The following day, Smith was leading a division of four Wildcats that clashed with Zero-sens near Savo Island. Having spotted six enemy fighters as they commenced their diving attack on his formation, Smith turned his division into the A6M2s and pulled up and fired at a Zero-sen as its pilot banked sharply away from him in order to avoid a head-on collision. Smith later claimed the fighter as destroyed. TSgt Johnny Lindley had to crash-land at Henderson after his Wildcat was badly shot up.

Two days later, Smith and his pilots were drawn into the Battle of the Eastern Solomons. The Japanese had rapidly gathered a significant number of troops to deal with the Americans on Guadalcanal. A combined Imperial Japanese Navy (IJN) and Imperial Japanese Army (IJA) landing force totaling 1,500 troops would be escorted to Guadalcanal, with the IJN's Combined Fleet, which included the carriers *Shokaku, Zuikaku,* and *Ryujo,* supporting the landings. With *Wasp* having been sent for refueling, Fletcher's TF 61 had TF 11 (centered around *Enterprise*) and TF 16 (including *Saratoga*) to do battle with the Japanese carriers, should they appear.

For two days, Japanese and American aircraft searched the seas around the Solomon Islands and the waters to the east for signs of enemy fleets. On the morning of August 24, a US Navy PBY Catalina spotted a Japanese carrier with escorts northeast of TF 61, but out of range of the American carrier-based aircraft, which would have to wait to launch a strike.

In the early afternoon, as part of the Japanese plan for the assault on Guadalcanal, the carrier *Ryujo* sent out six B5N2 Type 97 Carrier Attack Bombers ("Kate") with an escort of 15 Zero-sens to attack Henderson Field. The "Kates" would bomb horizontally, after which nine Zero-sens would drop down to strafe the airfield.

As the *Ryujo* force approached Guadalcanal, Capt Marion Carl was flying a CAP over the island with three other Wildcats. Having received word of the incoming raid, Henderson Field scrambled ten more Wildcats, which climbed for altitude. Carl duly attacked the IJNAF formation, shooting down what he thought was one of the bombers but was in fact a Zero-sen from the close escort. Carl then pulled up for a second attack and shot down one of the "Kates" in an overhead pass. His fellow pilots claimed two more bombers destroyed and seriously damaged a fourth that later ditched. Other Wildcat pilots shot down a second Zero-sen, and a third fell to two USAAF P-400 Airacobras. VMF-223 had three Wildcats shot down and two pilots killed. A fourth pilot ditched his damaged fighter near Florida Island, from where he was rescued by friendly islanders.

Later that afternoon the rival carrier forces went on the attack. Having located *Ryujo*, TF 61 sent out a strike force from *Saratoga* consisting of 29 SBDs from VB-3 and VS-3 and seven brand new TBF Avengers from VT-3. These aircraft so severely damaged *Ryujo* it had to be scuttled that night. Vice Adm Fletcher received conflicting reports on the location of *Shokaku* and *Zuikaku,* so he hesitated to send out a strike force. By then, however, IJNAF search aircraft had located *Enterprise* and *Saratoga*.

The Japanese carriers prepared their attack, sending out a first strike wave of 27 Type 99 carrier bombers from *Shokaku* and *Zuikaku*, with ten Zero-sens from the two carriers as escort. The second wave consisted of nine Type 99 carrier bombers and six Zero-sens from *Zuikaku*. Twenty-five Wildcats from VF-5 off *Saratoga* and 29 from VF-6 off *Enterprise* were on CAP or were scrambled to defend their carriers. In the intense and swirling combats that ensued around TF 61 that afternoon VF-5 claimed 14 Type 99s and three Zero-sens shot down, while VF-6 was credited with downing 12 Type 99s and 12 Zero-sens. Three pilots from VF-5 and two from VF-6 were shot down, with three more F4F-4s either forced to ditch or destroyed in crashes.

Actual Japanese losses were 17 Type 99s (ten from *Shokaku* and seven from *Zuikaku*) and four Zero-sens (one from *Shokaku* and three from *Zuikaku*), this aerial engagement resulting in a clear victory for the US Navy fighters. Nevertheless, *Enterprise* was damaged in the attack.

Two divisions from VF-6, led by Lt Albert Vorse and Lt(jg) Theodore Gay Jr, were credited with destroying nine Zero-sens between them without loss. During the combat several pilots claimed the same fighter, hence the high score, when in reality the divisions actually downed fewer Japanese aircraft through a combination of good tactics and accurate shooting.

Vorse was leading his division in a climb after the on-coming Type 99 bombers when Machinist Howell Sumrall noticed one of the escorting Zero-sens readying an attack on the Wildcats below him. He waited until the Zero-sen pilot, Seaman

Capt Marion Carl was the US Marine Corps' first ace, having claimed one Zero-sen over Midway and two B5N2 Type 97 Carrier Attack Bombers, another Zero-sen and a G4M Type 1 Land-based Attack Bomber on August 24, 1942. (Tony Holmes Collection)

1/c Shigeru Hayashi, dove down to attack. Knowing his opponent's likely tactics, Sumrall made a tight left turn to throw off Hayashi's aim, then reversed his turn as the Zero-sen flew past, letting off a short burst of fire to keep the fighter diving. As he recorded in his Aircraft Action Report:

> The Zero dove below me because of a short burst from my guns and pulled up after making a pass at me. This was the usual Zero tactic, and I was waiting for him to do this. As he came up I had a good shot at him and he crashed after a dive.

Apparently, Ens Francis Register also fired at this fighter, claiming it, too, as destroyed. Miraculously, Hayashi survived the encounter.

Register had made the mistake of following the Zero-sen down, and as he climbed back up he came under attack from one of three IJNAF fighters. He made a sharp turn to the right, then quickly turned to the left, forcing his opponent to overshoot in a turn to the left. Fortunately for Register, Lt(jg) Gay and his division spotted the F4F under attack and dove down to the rescue. Seeing the Wildcats diving down on him, the Zero-sen pilot made a climbing turn to the right followed by a sharp turn in the opposite direction, crossing directly in front of Gay's sights. The Naval Aviator opened fire and the Zero-sen burst into flames. Ens Charles Lindsay, following Gay, also fired at the aircraft and subsequently claimed it shot down.

In his Aircraft Action Report on his unit's experience and that of several VF-6 divisions launched from *Saratoga* during the battle on August 24, Lt Cdr Leroy Simpler, CO of VF-5, noted several positive comments from pilots who had engaged the Zero-sens. While acknowledging the continued overall superiority of the IJNAF fighter over the Wildcat, the tactics the US Navy pilots had employed against the Zero-sen had been effective. Interestingly, pilots felt that the F4F-4 was a match for or superior to the Zero-sen above 18,000ft, and they noted how during combat their opponents had shown a "decided disinclination" to attack sections of two F4F-4s and would not, or could not, follow a Wildcat in a radical corkscrew dive. Several pilots noticed that "the Zeros persist, to their usual sorrow, of making a steep stern attack and pulling up ahead and in range of the F4F-4."

The next clash between IJN and US Navy carriers would not take place until October 1942 during the Battle of Santa Cruz. Following the Battle of the Eastern Solomons, the IJNAF employed its land-based bombers and fighters, flying from Rabaul, to destroy American air units based on Guadalcanal in repeated attacks. IJN battleships, cruisers, and destroyers supplemented the daylight air raids with nighttime shelling of Henderson Field.

From the end of August until mid-November, when Japanese air attacks tapered off, five US Marine Corps Wildcat squadrons and one US Navy unit detached to Guadalcanal fought a sometimes desperate battle to protect the airfields and the dive- and torpedo-bombers attacking Japanese shipping. The F4F-4 Wildcat continued to see combat in the South Pacific after Guadalcanal was secured, serving with a declining number of US Marine Corps squadrons as they converted to the F4U Corsair and with US Navy fighter squadrons transferred to land bases from their carriers until the final F4F-4 combat missions were flown in July 1943.

CHAPTER 2
SETTING THE SCENE

Before World War II, few senior Japanese or American military officers could have predicted that the two nations would engage in a bitter fight for control of the Solomon Islands. The clash that began at Guadalcanal in August 1942 and continued for the next year-and-a-half had its origin in the re-evaluation of Japanese and American strategic objectives following Japan's lightning victories in Asia and the Central Pacific.

American strategy in the event of conflict with Japan was based on War Plan Orange, developed through many iterations in the decades before World War II. Basically, War Plan Orange called for a westward advance across the Pacific in three phases. Phase I would be defensive, probably involving the loss of the Philippines, while the US Navy mobilized the fleet and conducted probing raids against Japanese positions in its defensive line. Phase II would involve the westward advance to seize Japanese-held islands in Micronesia, wearing the enemy down through attritional battles and capturing bases in the Philippines and in the Marianas. In Phase III, US forces would advance to Japan, capturing the Ryukyus and bases on the Asian mainland to enforce an economic blockade of Japan with damaging air attacks on its industries, crippling the country's ability to make war.

Following Japan's attack on Pearl Harbor on December 7, 1941, and lightning victories throughout Southeast Asia, the basic premises underlying America's strategic plan for war with Japan changed dramatically. Not only had the Philippines been lost, but the Pacific Fleet had been badly damaged in the attack on Pearl Harbor. Furthermore, the US government had committed itself to a strategy of defeating Germany before Japan under the Rainbow Five plan.

The conditions the American military now faced were not what had been expected in Phase I of the pre-war Plan Orange. US forces were now part of an Allied coalition, fighting alongside Australian, British, Chinese, and New Zealand forces in Asia and the Pacific. The defensive area had expanded exponentially from the eastern Pacific ocean around Hawaii, the American West Coast, and the Panama Canal to encompass the islands in the South Pacific, New Zealand, and Australia, and further west to India.

A Liberty transport vessel unloads vital cargo in the Solomons. An objective of Japan's advance beyond Rabaul to Guadalcanal was to establish an air base that could threaten the line of communications between the USA and Australia. (80G-K-1241, RG80, NARA)

In the months following the attack on Pearl Harbor, the US military rushed what reinforcements of troops, aircraft, and ships that could be scraped together to the South Pacific to defend Australia, New Zealand, and major island groups – the New Hebrides, Fiji, Samoa, New Caledonia, and other smaller islands. In the months before Pearl Harbor, a primitive air route had been established across the Pacific from the American West Coast to Australia, with stops on small islands along the way. This air and sea line of communication now had to be defended.

In April 1942, the American Joint Chiefs of Staff created theater commands for the war against Japan, designating Adm Chester Nimitz as commander of the Pacific Theater (POA) that was divided into North Pacific (NORPAC), Central Pacific (CENPAC), and South Pacific (SOPAC) areas. The Southwest Pacific Command (SOWESPAC), under the command of Gen Douglas MacArthur (who had been withdrawn from the Philippines), took on responsibility for the defense of Australia and New Guinea. The debate that followed was over where and how the Allies, once Australia and New Zealand were secure, should begin the counter-offensive against Japan.

While the US Navy favored the westward advance across the Pacific, MacArthur proposed using Australia as a base for an advance through New Guinea to retake the Philippines. But this advance would have to deal with the Japanese position at Rabaul, in the Bismarck archipelago. Rabaul needed to be eliminated to protect the right flank of MacArthur's planned advance. Allied intelligence had also followed Japanese activities in the Solomon Islands south of Rabaul, where the IJN had established a seaplane base at Tulagi, a small island north of Guadalcanal. Japanese intentions to expand its presence further with an airfield on Guadalcanal in addition to the base at Tulagi triggered an

This aerial photograph of the airfield on Guadalcanal was taken shortly after its capture by the US Marine Corps. The large clump of trees at the top of the image had to be removed to make the airfield safer for landings and take-offs. The airfield remained in a rough state for several months, and operational accidents were frequent as a result. (80G-10546, RG80, NARA)

immediate American response. The Japanese had to be stopped from building an airfield that could threaten the islands to the south of the Solomons and the air and sea routes between America and Australia.

Japan also faced a dilemma in deciding on strategic objectives. Its strategy had been to seize the resources in Southeast Asia needed to sustain the country's war industries and set up a defensive perimeter around its conquests, then make it prohibitively expensive in men and resources for the Allies to breach this barrier. The question facing Japan's Imperial Headquarters was defining the extent of the defensive barrier.

In looking at the South Pacific, the IJN's pre-war planners had recognized the need to capture a position in the Bismarck Archipelago to defend the major IJN base at Truk, in the Caroline Islands. In January 1942, Japanese forces had seized Rabaul, on New Britain, which had both an excellent harbor and space for airfields. Capturing Rabaul, however, created a need to protect this new base, resulting in a decision to extend Japan's offensive barrier to New Guinea and the Solomon Islands. In May, Japanese forces captured the small Australian seaplane base on the island of Tulagi.

After the IJA had categorically rejected a plan to invade Australia, the IJN came up with a compromise to capture Fiji and Samoa in order to disrupt the lines of communication between the USA and Australia. Designated Operation *FS*, it had to be postponed after the IJN's defeat during the Battle of Midway and was subsequently canceled. The IJN, however, believed that even with the cancelation of the operation, there remained a need to strengthen what was now called the "Outer South Seas" defensive perimeter. Tulagi would become a base for long-range IJNAF flying boats which could scout far to the south. Building an airfield on nearby Guadalcanal would provide a base for

Capt Harold W. "Joe" Bauer was widely regarded as perhaps the US Marine Corps' finest aviator pre-war. Whilst CO of VMF-212, he claimed 11 victories (eight of them in just two sorties) and had attained the rank of lieutenant colonel prior to being posted Missing in Action on November 14, 1942. (Tony Holmes Collection)

OPPOSITE
IJNAF Zero-sen pilots had to fly long distances (an 1,120-mile round trip from their base at Rabaul) for much of the Guadalcanal campaign, whereas F4F units of the Cactus Air Force often flew CAP and interception missions directly over Henderson Field. Australian coastwatchers regularly provided radio warnings of impending raids to the Wildcat squadrons, enabling their pilots to gain altitude in time to intercept incoming IJNAF formations.

land attack bombers for future operations with the IJN's Combined Fleet in attacks on Allied bases and shipping to the south. The IJN transferred two construction units to Guadalcanal in July, and they immediately began building an airfield.

The American military was already considering an offensive in the Solomon Islands. MacArthur wanted to assault Rabaul directly, but Adm Ernst King, Chief of Naval Operations, argued successfully for a more limited offensive against the Japanese base at Tulagi. When Allied intelligence identified Japanese activity on Guadalcanal, plans shifted to capturing that island as well as Tulagi in Operation *Watchtower*. Vice Adm Robert Ghormley, SOPAC commander, hurriedly arranged for the 1st Marine Division to seize Guadalcanal, with support from TF 61 and its carriers *Enterprise, Saratoga,* and *Wasp*.

On August 7, 1942, the US Marine Corps landed on Guadalcanal and quickly captured the crude airfield the Japanese were still constructing, soon to be named Henderson Field in honor of Marine Maj Lofton Henderson who had been killed at Midway, while carrier aircraft bombed the Japanese seaplane base at Tulagi and provided air cover for the invasion force. This was the beginning of a brutal battle of attrition on air, land, and sea that lasted until February 8, 1943, when the Japanese completed their withdrawal from Guadalcanal.

The air battles over Guadalcanal were the Wildcat's finest hour. For six months US Marine Corps and US Navy F4F pilots, together with their USAAF counterparts, fought experienced IJNAF pilots in their superlative A6M Zero-sens – an aircraft that was superior to the Wildcat in virtually all respects. In his study of aerial combat in the South Pacific, titled *Fire in the Sky*, Eric Bergerud includes a quote from Lt Col "Joe" Bauer comparing the Zero-sen and the Wildcat. Bauer apparently said to the US Marine Corps pilots of what came to be called the Cactus Air Force after the code name for the airfield on Guadalcanal, "A Zero can go faster than you can, it climbs faster than you can, and it can outmaneuver you. Aside from those things, you've got a better airplane."

Wildcat pilots had to develop tactics that would take advantage of the aircraft's strengths, and learn how to protect themselves when attacked. The US Marine Corps and US Navy fighter pilots flying over Guadalcanal had two objectives: to defend their airfield against Japanese attack and defend the dive- and torpedo-bombers going after IJN shipping bringing supplies and reinforcements to the Japanese troops fighting on the island.

In this, the F4F pilots were successful, but at a cost. In the fighting over Guadalcanal, US Marine Corps squadrons lost 94 pilots killed or missing in action, while the US Navy squadrons that participated in the carrier battles off the Solomons and from Guadalcanal had 31 pilots killed. US Marine Corps pilots claimed 427 Japanese aircraft shot down during the campaign, with US Navy squadrons claiming an additional 193 destroyed. The actual total was no doubt far less, but the key point is that Japanese air power failed to dislodge American forces from Guadalcanal.

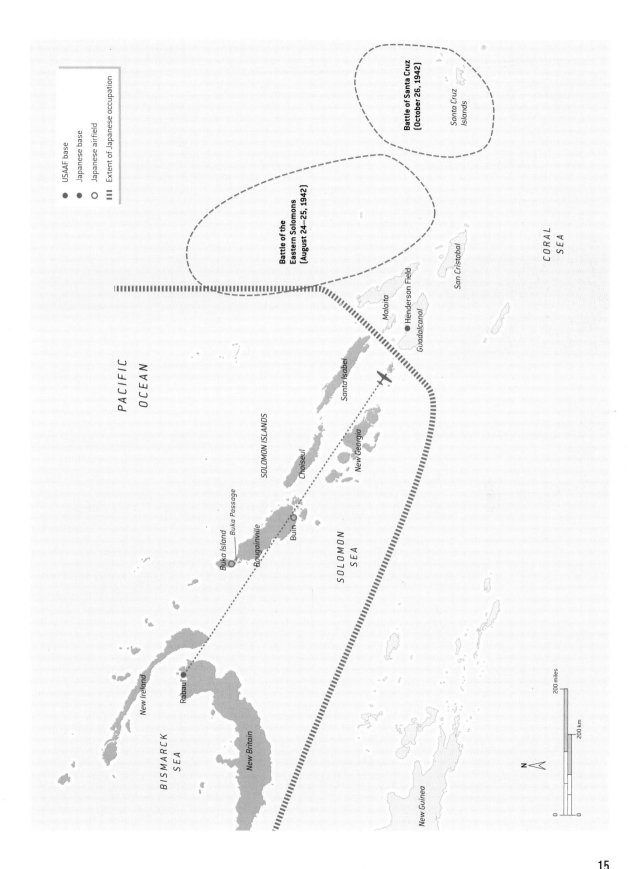

USAAF base
Japanese base
Japanese airfield
Extent of Japanese occupation

Battle of Santa Cruz
(October 26, 1942)

Santa Cruz
Islands

Battle of the
Eastern Solomons
(August 24–25, 1942)

CORAL
SEA

Malaita

Henderson Field
Guadalcanal

San Cristobal

PACIFIC
OCEAN

Santa Isabel

SOLOMON ISLANDS

Choiseul

New Georgia

Buka Island
Buka Passage

Bougainville

Buin

SOLOMON
SEA

New Ireland

Rabaul

BISMARCK
SEA

New Britain

New Guinea

N

0   200 miles
0   200 km

15

The Wildcat's role in the South Pacific did not end at Guadalcanal, but continued on for another six months. While US Marine Corps F4F squadrons progressively re-equipped with the more capable F4U Corsair, US Navy Wildcat pilots continued to fly the Grumman fighter in combat for several more months after Guadalcanal had been declared secured. Moreover, the US Navy assigned several F4F squadrons to Guadalcanal to support the slow slog up the Solomons chain toward Rabaul, these units seeing their last action during July 1943. These combats were just as fierce as the earlier battles over Guadalcanal, and the squadrons involved continued to suffer losses at the hands of IJNAF Zero-sen pilots till the very end of the Wildcat's service in the theater.

The character of the air war changed as the campaign in the Solomons progressed. In the initial desperate months after the landings on Guadalcanal, Henderson Field and the adjacent "Fighter One" airstrip could accommodate only two US Marine Corps squadrons and a detached US Navy Wildcat squadron, as well as a small number of USAAF P-39s and P-400s. There were often less than two-dozen F4Fs available to engage the incoming Japanese air raids, and sometimes fewer. More often than not, IJNAF fighters and bombers outnumbered the Wildcats.

After the withdrawal of the last Japanese troops on Guadalcanal in early February, the F4F squadrons found themselves increasingly escorting US Marine Corps and US Navy SBDs and TBFs in their attacks on IJN shipping and Japanese positions along the Solomon Islands chain. Air combat with Japanese fighters and bombers now involved many more aircraft, with US Marine Corps Corsairs and, later, USAAF P-38 Lightnings and P-40 Warhawks and Royal New Zealand Air Force (RNZAF) Kittyhawks joining the Wildcat squadrons.

Establishing airfields and expanding the area of fighter coverage, and denying the Japanese similar bases, proved critical to the Allied advance against the enemy in the South and Southwest Pacific.

With Guadalcanal secure, Allied planners turned to the next steps in what Adm King called the "defensive–offensive" phase of the war in the Pacific. It became clear that in order for MacArthur to advance in New Guinea and for the US Navy to eliminate the IJN naval fortress at Truk in support of operations in the Central Pacific, the Allies would have to neutralize the base at Rabaul. With the resources that could be made available to SOPAC, this meant a slow slog up the Solomon Islands chain toward the Bismarck archipelago – an advance that the Japanese in the northern Solomons resisted fiercely.

The IJNAF continued to funnel in units and aircraft to contest Allied efforts to establish air control over the Solomons, and built airfields on the islands of New Georgia and Bougainville, closer to Allied bases in the southern Solomons. In late February 1943, the US Marine Corps and US Army occupied the Russell Islands in the first advance beyond Guadalcanal. A month later, the US Navy commissioned a new airfield, pushing air operations farther up the Solomons toward Bougainville. On June 30, the US Marine Corps and US Army commenced the invasion of New Georgia with the aim of capturing the Japanese airfield at Munda, which, after a lengthy and difficult fight and a hurried construction effort that followed, was ready for Corsair squadrons in August.

The Allies had steadily expanded the number of aircraft in-theater for combat over the Solomons from the dark days of 1942. To support the landings on New

Georgia, they had some 533 aircraft based at Guadalcanal and Russell Island. On the day of the landings, there were 213 fighters and 170 dive- and torpedo-bombers available – a far cry from the desperate months of September–October 1942. In aerial battles over New Georgia in July 1943, more than 100 US Marine Corps, US Navy, USAAF, and RNZAF fighters engaged in the fighting.

During June–July, US Navy squadrons operating from Guadalcanal made the final Wildcat claims in the South Pacific. To the very end of F4F operations, the Zero-sen remained a formidable opponent. In June 1943, the US Navy Wildcat units had lost 15 aircraft in aerial combat with Japanese fighters, and during the F4F's last significant clash with enemy aircraft in the South Pacific, on July 18, 1943, six Naval Aviators failed to return.

As Eric Bergerud has observed, aerial fighting over the Solomons took place in what he terms "an unimaginably hostile environment" for both sides. There was, as he comments, a "razor-thin edge between survival and oblivion." Pilots had to cope with weather and crudely built airfields, often short rations, nighttime shelling from IJN vessels, disease, and many threats to survival if they were forced to bail out over jungle or ocean. Allied fighter pilots at least had the benefit of friendly islanders, who at great risk to themselves rescued countless pilots and brought them to safety, as well as aircraft and warships that could effect a rescue when Australian coastwatchers notified Allied commands that a downed airman had been spotted. Japanese aviators were not so fortunate.

Pilots flew frequently, being tasked with numerous missions aside from intercepting Japanese air raids. For certain periods, the Wildcat squadrons on Henderson Field carried out dawn and dusk patrols. Incoming and outgoing air transport and Allied shipping also needed to be covered, US Marine Corps and US Navy dive- and torpedo-bombers required a fighter escort and the Wildcats often joined in attacking Japanese shipping sailing in the "Slot," as the passage down the Solomons chain came to be called. All this was wearing on aviators. Of the 464 US Marine Corps pilots who flew during the battle for Guadalcanal, 177 were evacuated as casualties due to wounds, sickness, or exhaustion.

During the early months of aerial combat over Guadalcanal, US Marine Corps and US Navy Wildcat pilots were fortunate in that they could often land their damaged aircraft back at Henderson Field, while their IJNAF counterparts had to struggle on the long flight over open water back to Rabaul. (127GW-897I-61572, RG127, NARA)

CHAPTER 3
PATH TO COMBAT

In the late 1930s, the growing risk of war transformed the US Navy's approach to pilot training. Until 1940 it had fewer than 2,000 active Naval Aviators, and trained only a few hundred per year, drawing its candidates from graduates of the US Naval Academy, civilians who entered through the V-5 Naval Aviation Cadet Program, established in 1935, and a small number from within the ranks of serving US Navy officers and enlisted men. With authorization from the United States Congress for only a limited number of aircraft and pilots, the goal of the US Navy's aviation training was to produce versatile pilots who would be able to fly any type of aircraft in the inventory. During their flying career, Naval Aviators could thus be assigned to carrier or land-based squadrons depending on requirements.

Most prospective civilian candidates who entered the US Navy through the Naval Aviation Cadet Program, having completed the required years of college education, received 30 days of elimination training at one of 12 Naval Air Reserve Bases across the country. Instructors taught recruits basic flying skills in N3N "Yellow Peril" biplane trainers in order to determine their suitability as pilots, candidates receiving 15 hours of dual instruction before logging one hour of solo flying. If successful, the candidate went on to Pensacola, Florida, considered the home of naval aviation, where, as an aviation cadet, he would spend 33 weeks in ground school and undertake a year of flight training.

Prior to October 1939, aviation cadets at Pensacola worked their way through five squadrons during their year of training. Cadets spent nine weeks in Squadron One, where they learned to fly primary seaplanes (N3Ns with floats), practicing all basic flying maneuvers. In Squadron Two, the cadets spent 18 weeks flying primary land aircraft (N3Ns or N2Ss), where they were introduced to formation, cross-country, and night flying. The cadets then spent nine weeks in Squadron Three flying more powerful O3U and SU observation aircraft, repeating all the maneuvers they had learned on their primary trainers.

The next stage was nine weeks in Squadron Four, where cadets learned to fly large P3M and P2Y flying boats, with a short course in flying floatplanes from a catapult. The final stage of training was Squadron Five, where cadets flew recent service fighter, dive-, and torpedo-bomber aircraft. They also practiced carrier landings for the first time, as well as gunnery, dive-bombing, and instrument flying in new SNJ trainers.

From 1938, cadets who completed their training successfully were commissioned as ensigns in the US Navy or second lieutenants in the US Marine Corps and went on to squadron assignments, having accumulated around 300 hours of flying time. Many of the senior Wildcat pilots who fought in the South Pacific – men like US Navy pilots Lt Cdr Jimmy Flatley and Lt Stanley Vejtasa, and the US Marine Corps' Majs Robert Galer and John Smith and Capt Marion Carl – went through all or most of this early flight training program.

In October 1939, after the outbreak of war in Europe, the US Navy revised its aviation training program to increase the number of pilots being produced. It now needed to train the maximum number of Naval Aviators in the minimum amount of time. The US Navy condensed ground school to 18 weeks and abandoned the five squadron system, shortening flying training from a year to six months. Going forward,

A sailor closes the panel in the forward fuselage of an N3N-1 after helping crank the biplane's Wright J-5 radial engine into life at the start of a training flight for a Naval Aviation cadet, circa 1940–42. Nicknamed the "Yellow Peril," the Naval Aircraft Factory N3N served as the primary trainer for the US Navy and US Marine Corps from 1936. It shared this role with the more common Stearman NS/N2S, the first examples of which entered service with the US Navy in 1935. (Tony Holmes Collection)

After completing their Primary and Basic intermediate training phases, Naval Aviation cadets selected for fleet fighter units moved on to fly the Curtiss SNC and the North American SNJ in the Advanced intermediate training syllabus. (80G-472821, RG80, NARA)

aviation cadets would receive their Primary training on the N3N or N2S landplanes and their Basic intermediate training, including instrument flying, in new monoplane trainers like the SNV. The latter served as a bridge to the advanced training phase, where cadets specialized in patrol or utility aircraft, observation types, or carrier aircraft (fighters and dive- and torpedo-bombers).

This revision in the training regime proved timely, for in July 1940, as US forces began to benefit from a somewhat belated rearmament program, the US Navy received approval from Congress to increase its authorized aircraft strength to 15,000, requiring a significant expansion in pilots and aircrew to fly them. At the same time, Congress appropriated funds to build 12 new naval air stations, including a major new training center at Corpus Christi on the Gulf Coast of Texas.

To streamline training even further, in July 1941 the US Navy abolished the requirement that pilots destined for service on carriers had to master the three basic carrier aircraft types, and instead started assigning students to specialize in fighters, dive-, or torpedo-bombers.

In the prewar system, new graduates of Pensacola received training in operational methods and tactics once they joined their squadrons. To relieve the latter of this burden, in July 1941 the US Navy formed Advanced Carrier Training Groups (ACTGs) to take over operational training. At the ACTGs, new pilots were to receive additional training in operational flying, covering

Three F4F-3s of VMF-111 participate in the large-scale joint service maneuvers that were staged across the southern USA in 1941. The red crosses indicate that the Wildcats belonged to the "Red Force," opposing the friendly "Blue Force," whose aircraft were marked with white crosses. Naval Aviators who completed their flying training during 1941 were fortunate to have more time to build up their flying hours on the F4F than those who received their wings the following year. (Tony Holmes Collection)

combat tactics, gunnery, carrier qualifications, and additional instruction in navigation and night flying. After the start of the war, and for some months thereafter, shortages of instructors and modern combat aircraft limited what new pilots could learn at the ACTGs.

Between 1941 and 1942, the number of Naval Aviators increased nearly three-fold as the training effort ramped up to fill newly established carrier- and land-based units. In his study of US Navy fighter squadrons in combat in the Pacific in 1942, John Lundstrom estimated that pilots who received their wings during 1941 had accumulated between 300 and 600 hours of flying time prior to entering combat, while those who received their wings during 1942 had around 300 flying hours – half of what their Japanese opponents would have had.

As a result, many US Navy and US Marine Corps Wildcat squadrons that entered combat in the South Pacific contained a few experienced senior officer and enlisted pilots, but mostly new ensigns and second lieutenants who had only completed their training during 1942. VMF-121, for example, arrived on Guadalcanal on October 12, 1942 with 22 second lieutenants out of 28 pilots.

The experiences of Edward L. Feightner and Jefferson DeBlanc, both future Wildcat aces, as they moved through the US Navy's training system and on to combat squadrons, are representative of the many newly-minted pilots who went to war during 1942.

Feightner, from Ohio, and DeBlanc, from Louisiana, had both learned to fly through the Civilian Pilot Training Program and enlisted in the US Navy in the summer of 1941. After passing their initial ground school and elimination flight training, they were assigned to Naval Air Station Corpus Christi as members of Class 10B 41C. Benefiting from their previous training,

An F4F-4 of VMF-121 during work-ups at Camp Kearney, north of San Diego, in the summer of 1942. The unit was mainly staffed by inexperienced aviators, with 22 of its 28-strong pilot cadre being second lieutenants when the unit reached Guadalcanal on October 12, 1942. Thanks to the thoroughness of their training, this proved no barrier in combat, however, with VMF-121 claiming more than 160 aerial victories through to April 1943, when the unit replaced its F4F-4s with F4U-1s. (Tony Holmes Collection)

In the early months of the war a shortage of frontline fighters meant that newly fledged pilots had to do their operational training on obsolete biplanes like the F3F-3, a delightful aircraft to fly, but not a modern monoplane fighter. Ens Edward Feightner and 2Lt Jefferson DeBlanc, who were both in the same training class, flew the F3F-3 on multiple occasions. (72-AC-18D-3, RG72, NARA)

Feightner and DeBlanc had no problem getting through their primary training phase in N2Ns and N2Ss, where they were introduced to aerobatics and the precision flying the US Navy required of its pilots.

Moving on to intermediate training, both pilots flew the SNV Valiant, SNC and OS2U Kingfisher, gaining experience in more powerful monoplanes. Feightner and DeBlanc did well in their training, and to their relief both received their choice of flying fighters for the second, advanced phase of their intermediate training. However, in the spring of 1942, active squadrons had first claim on the newer F2A and F4F-3 Wildcat fighters, so Feightner and DeBlanc trained on the older and now obsolete F3F-3. In his memoir of his flying experiences during the war, DeBlanc described his delight in flying the portly biplane:

I cannot describe the thrill I felt as I poured the coal to the little Grumman biplane. The plane leaped into the air in seconds, and it took me just a few more seconds to control all those "horses" running wild under the cowling. I flew the familiarization hop for half-an-hour, doing the usual maneuvers, but my thoughts were on the machine gun levers hanging on the control stick. I even looked through the gunsight and could "see" the Red Baron ahead of me. Two levers had to be jackknifed parallel with the control stick before firing the guns. One controlled the 0.50-cal. machine gun and the other controlled the 0.30-cal. machine gun. Both guns fired through the propeller. But the revolutions of the propeller had to be above 1,000rpm or there would be danger of shooting it off. A telescopic tubular gunsight penetrated the windscreen.

It must have been quite a task to fly and fight at the same time. If you failed to fly smoothly and were skidding slightly, the machine gun bullets would take off on a tangent to your flight path and you would miss the target. Hence, smooth flying during training was emphasized. As cadets, we learned to ignore this obsolete gunsight and fire the guns at the towed sleeve by "feel." We got more hits this way. The gunnery phase passed with little trouble for most of us. Those who failed this part were taken out of fighters and placed in twin-engined aircraft or dive-bombers.

Edward Feightner received his commission as an ensign in April 1942 and joined VF-10 six months later. When he reached his squadron he had accumulated 323 hours of military flying time. Feightner made his initial claims during the Battle of Santa Cruz on October 26, 1942, and on January 30, 1943, was credited with three "Betty" bombers shot down. He finished the war with nine victories to his name, and eventually attained the rank of rear admiral. (80G-39595, RG80, NARA)

Feightner received his commission as an ensign on April 3, 1942, while DeBlanc became a second lieutenant in the US Marine Corps on May 4. From this point their experiences diverged. With the shortening of schedules, Feightner and DeBlanc completed their flight training with less than 300 hours of flying time. Feightner checked out in the Wildcat, before heading to the West Coast to join VF-5, then embarked in USS *Yorktown* (CV-5). However, the vessel was sunk in the Battle of Midway before he reached the unit.

The US Navy duly transferred Feightner to VF-3, in Hawaii, under the command of Lt Cdr "Butch" O'Hare, where he began intensive practice in aerial combat and gunnery. Instead of remaining with the squadron, Feightner was posted to newly-formed VF-10 when its CO, Lt Cdr Jimmy Flatley, needed replacements for several pilots lost in the squadron's work-up period prior to joining *Enterprise* and heading for the South Pacific.

After receiving his wings and commission, DeBlanc was assigned to the Advanced Carrier Training Group in San Diego, California, spending the summer flying SNJ trainers and attending photo school. On September 28, 1942, DeBlanc checked out in the F4F-3 and on October 2 joined his first squadron, VMF-112. Before he could get much flying time with the unit, VMF-112 shipped out to the Pacific theater, leaving San Diego on October 10. When he went off to combat, DeBlanc had just ten hours in the F4F and had received no gunnery or night flying training in the Wildcat. After a short stay in Nouméa, on New Caledonia, DeBlanc arrived on Guadalcanal on November 10, 1942, and was in combat the next day.

CHAPTER 4
WEAPON OF WAR

Perhaps surprisingly, the Grumman Wildcat began life as a biplane. In the mid-1930s, the availability of air-cooled radial engines of greater horsepower, retractable landing gear, variable-pitch propellers, all-metal construction, and the resulting aerodynamic refinements presaged greatly improved performance over the biplane carrier aircraft then in service.

In 1934 the US Navy had issued contracts to Douglas Aircraft, Chance Vought, Northrop, and Brewster for prototypes of all-metal monoplane scout bomber and torpedo-bomber aircraft. A year later, in November 1935, it solicited designs for a new carrier fighter. Grumman proposed the XF4F-1, a biplane along the lines of the company's F3F-1, with the same manually retractable landing gear. Powered by a Pratt & Whitney R-1535 14-cylinder, double-row, air-cooled radial engine offering 800hp, the XF4F-1 promised a maximum speed of 264mph.

Events soon caused Grumman to abandon the XF4F-1 in favor of a newer, more modern monoplane design. The company's own studies had shown that when fitted with the Wright R-1820 air-cooled radial engine of 950hp to 1,000hp, the older F3F-1 could achieve a performance that nearly matched the XF4F-1. This became the basis for the F3F-2 and later F3F-3. More critically, in June 1936, Brewster was awarded a contract for its XF2A monoplane fighter.

Grumman's response was the XF4F-2, a mid-wing monoplane with an all-metal wing, manually

The XF4F-2 was Grumman's entry for the US Navy's Bureau of Aeronautics' competition for a new carrier fighter. The aircraft, which made its first flight in September 1937, was beaten by the Brewster Corporation's XF2A. However, the US Navy encouraged Grumman to continue development of its fighter. (72-AC-18E-9, RG72, NARA)

The XF4F-3 featured a more powerful Pratt & Whitney engine and squared-off wings, horizontal stabilizers, and vertical tail. Armament comprised two 0.30-cal. machine guns firing through the propeller and two wing-mounted 0.50-cal. machine guns. This was an improvement over the standard twin 0.30-cal. machine guns fitted in the earlier F2F and the single 0.30-cal. and 0.50-cal. weapons in the F3F. (80G-2885, RG80, NARA)

retractable landing gear and armament of two 0.50-cal. nose-mounted machine guns firing through the propeller. Grumman changed the powerplant on its design to the Pratt & Whitney R-1830 Twin Wasp engine – a double-row, 14-cylinder, air-cooled radial engine that offered 1,050hp for take-off. With a single-stage, single-speed supercharger, the R-1830 provided 900hp at 12,000ft, giving the XF4F-2 a maximum speed of 288mph.

Although Grumman lost the initial contract to Brewster, the US Navy decided to pursue the company's promising design. Grumman revised the XF4F-2 into the XF4F-3, with squared wingtips on wings of a larger span than those fitted to the XF4F-2, a squared-off rudder, and a more powerful Pratt & Whitney R-1830-76 engine with a two-speed, two-stage supercharger giving 1,200hp for take-off and 1,000hp at 19,000ft. This raised the maximum speed of the fighter to 336mph, making it faster than the F2A. The improved performance resulted in Grumman being awarded a contract for 54 F4F-3s in August 1939.

The first two F4F-3s built were armed with a pair of 0.30-cal. machine guns in the nose and two 0.50-cal machine guns in the wings, but this was soon changed to four 0.50-cal. weapons in the wings with the capacity of up to 430 rounds per gun, for a total of 1,720 rounds. Pilots flying early-build Wildcats aimed these weapons with older telescopic sights, but toward the end of 1941, the US Navy began fitting Mk 8 reflector gunsights into its F4F-3s.

Lacking sufficient R-1830s with two-stage superchargers, the F4F-3A used a single-stage supercharged version of the engine that had less performance at altitude. Many of the F4F-3As built went to US Marine Corps squadrons. By December 1941, the F4F-3/3A equipped ten US Navy and US Marine Corps squadrons, and this was the first version to see combat with these units in the opening months of the Pacific War in the ill-fated defense of Wake Island, supporting early carrier strikes in February 1942 and participating in the Battle of the Coral Sea three months later.

The next version of the Wildcat put into production was the F4F-4, which had been developed to meet a US Navy requirement for a folding wing on its carrier fighters. Grumman developed an ingenious manual folding mechanism that reduced the Wildcat's wingspan from 38ft to just 14ft, allowing carriers to

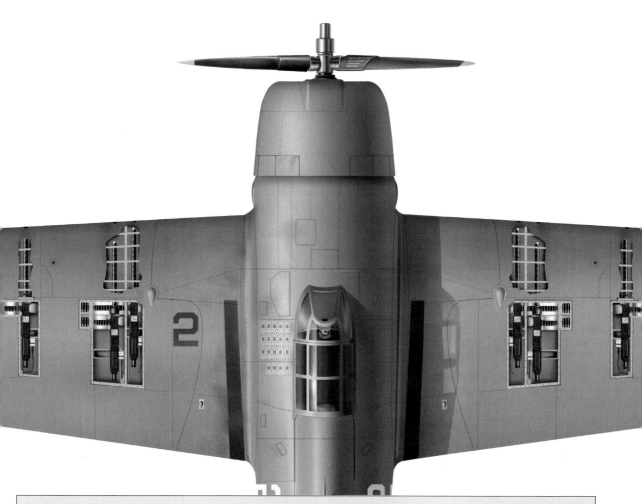

F4F-4 ARMAMENT

The F4F-4 was equipped with six 0.50-cal. Browning M2 machine guns, three in each wing, with 240 rounds for each weapon. This gave the pilot around 20 seconds of firing time at a rate of fire of 750–850 rounds per minute. Although the Zero-sen's Type 99-1 20mm cannon fired a heavier cartridge than the Wildcat's 0.50-cal. round, the F4F-4's six machine guns put out a heavier weight of fire than the A6M's two Type 99-1 20mm cannon and two Type 97 7.7mm machine guns. A two-second burst from the Wildcat's six guns was about 60 percent heavier than a two-second burst from a Zero-sen, and, if on target, could be devastating against the more lightly built IJNAF fighter and its unprotected fuel tanks. Some US Navy pilots stated a preference for the F4F-3's armament of just four 0.50-cal. machine guns, but with 450 rounds per gun.

accommodate more fighters. The F4F-4 added an additional 0.50-cal. machine in each wing, but with a reduced ammunition load of 1,440 rounds, or 240 rounds per gun. Based on experience in the air war over Europe, the F4F-4 carried 150lb of armor plate near the oil tank ahead of the cockpit and behind the pilot's seat and was fitted with a 27lb bullet-resistant laminated glass windshield as well as self-sealing fuel tanks.

The additional guns and protection for pilot and fuel added weight to the Wildcat, such that the gross weight of the F4F-4 was some 30 percent greater than the F4F-3. With no increase in horsepower from the R-1830, performance deteriorated, with the F4F-4 having a lower maximum speed and a lower ceiling than the F4F-3 – a development that did not find favor with many Naval Aviators.

Fortunately for the many newly-trained US Navy and US Marine Corps pilots commencing their squadron service, the Wildcat was a straightforward aircraft to fly, being ruggedly built and with few idiosyncrasies. It demonstrated excellent handling at low speeds, critical for landing on the deck of a carrier. Legendary Royal Navy Fleet Air Arm test pilot Capt Eric Brown considered the Wildcat to have "the best landing characteristics of any naval aircraft that I flew."

The structure of the aircraft was in some respects over-designed, much to the benefit of its pilots who would come to use sharp reversals in direction at high speeds to escape from the more maneuverable A6M Zero-sen. During a wartime test flight, a Grumman test pilot inadvertently registered a pullout of 12.5G – equal to the Wildcat's designed breaking load – during a terminal velocity dive, yet the aircraft held together to his relief and astonishment. The F4F and its Pratt & Whitney engine could absorb considerable punishment and survive. High-scoring IJNAF Zero-sen ace Saburo Sakai noted in his memoir his astonishment as to how, on his first encounter with the Wildcat over Guadalcanal in early August 1942, his opponent seemed to absorb more than 200 7.7mm rounds without apparent effect.

Corwin "Corky" Meyer, a long-time Grumman test pilot, recalled that the Wildcat had four built-in "bear traps" as he called them. The first was the high torque from the R-1830 engine that tended to pull a Wildcat off to the left on take-off and which had to be corrected with heavy right rudder. This was less of a problem for short take-offs from carriers, but was a concern in taking

The least liked feature of the F4F was the manually cranked landing gear, shown here just to the front of the pilot's seat. Naval Aviators had to make 31 turns of the landing gear crank to bring up the wheels after take-off, and then repeat the process to lower the gear for landing. This proved particularly annoying to F6F Hellcat and F4U Corsair pilots subsequently assigned to fly the later FM-2 from escort carriers. (72-AC-19A-48, RG72, NARA)

off from runways. Pilots new to the Wildcat were admonished to set the rudder trim tab on the Wildcat to the right to counter the torque.

Meyer considered the Wildcat's manual landing gear retraction system as another "bear trap." With the landing gear crank located on the right side of the cockpit, after take-off a pilot would have to remove his left hand from the throttle to take control of the stick, and use his right hand to make the 31 turns required to bring up the landing gear, reversing the process for landing.

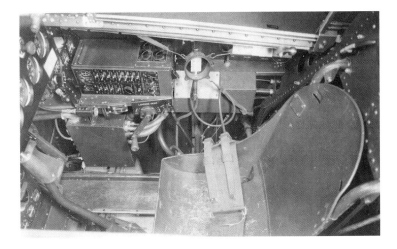

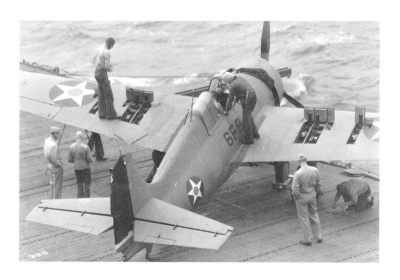

The other significant change with the F4F-4 was the increase of its armament to six 0.50-cal. machine guns, three in each wing. The added weight of the weaponry and armor protection for the pilot reduced the F4F-4's performance compared to the lighter F4F-3. (80G-14511, RG80, NARA)

There were also problems with the Wildcat's Curtiss Electric propeller in certain climatic conditions. Lastly, the Wildcat's narrow undercarriage and weak brakes made it subject to ground looping if the tail wheel was not locked and the rudder tab not set to counter the engine torque. In his memoir of his days testing Grumman aircraft, Meyer related a US Navy saying that there were two kinds of Wildcat pilots, "those who had ground looped it and those who were about to."

The Wildcat's performance against the Zero-sen in the battles of the Coral Sea and Midway caused a controversy among senior US Navy officers. Lt Cdr John Thach, who commanded VF-3 during Midway, wrote a scathing report, noting the F4F-4's deficiencies in climb, speed, and maneuverability compared to the Zero-sen. Thach said:

> It is indeed surprising that any of our pilots returned alive. Any success our fighter pilots may have had against the Japanese Zero fighter is *not* due to the performance of the airplane we fly but is the result of the comparatively poor marksmanship of the Japanese, stupid mistakes made by a few of their pilots, and superior marksmanship and team work by some of our pilots. The only way we can ever bring our guns to bear on the Zero fighter is to trick them into recovering in front of an F4F, or shoot them when they are preoccupied in firing at one of our own planes.

After encountering the Zero-sen during the Coral Sea fighting, Lt Cdr James Flatley, commanding VF-42, took a contrary view to his good friend Thach. Flatley believed that the Wildcat could more than hold its own against the IJNAF fighter if flown properly and the right tactics were used. Commenting on Thach's report, Flatley praised the F4F-4's armament, fuel tank protection, and greater strength, arguing that:

> Our planes and our pilots, if properly handled, are more than a match for the enemy. Let's not condemn our equipment. It shoots the enemy down in flames and gets most of us back to our base. Remember the mission of the fighter plane, the enemy's VF mission, is the same as our own. Work out tactics on that basis. We should be able to outsmart him.

Fortunately for the many young Naval Aviators who encountered the Zero-sen in their Wildcats in the months following the Battle of Midway, Thach and Flatley devised defensive and offensive tactics that would be proven to work when engaging the IJNAF fighter in aerial combat.

VMF-121's 2Lts Roger Haberman and Thomas Furlow both saw action in the defense of Guadalcanal, and they gave their opinions of the Wildcat to Eric

Bergerud for his book *Fire in the Sky*. In Haberman's view, shifting an aircraft designed for operating from carriers to land bases was not without its challenges:

> The Wildcat was not well suited for the fight at Guadalcanal. It has a bunch of weight in the back that we could have dispensed with very nicely. It was beefed up for carrier landings in the rear and we didn't need it. But there wasn't anything to be done in that regard. So, because of this weight, we'd work like hell to climb to 23,000–24,000ft. At that altitude, when you make a turn you lose 1,000ft, and it's very easy to stall out. You'd look up and there sat the Japs at 30,000ft, looking right down your gazoo. A real fun time. You couldn't get that bird much higher than 24,000ft – not you, not Jesus, nobody. The bird wouldn't go any higher.

The essential yet unheralded aspect of aviation is maintenance. This Marine is working on an R-1830-76 double-row, 14-cylinder, air-cooled radial engine fitted to an F4F-4 at Guadalcanal in 1942. (Tony Holmes Collection)

Furlow had more praise for the Wildcat's good points. As he recalled:

> The Wildcat was a simple plane. You didn't really have to monitor much. The air-cooled engine was a real advantage. I saw many planes that came in that had been hit, cylinders missing, shot off. And the plane got back. An inline engine went down fast if the coolant was damaged. And you had to crank the landing gear up by hand. It was hard to fly formation and crank the thing – you'd be looking down for the crank and looking around at the other aircraft. And later you had to crank it down. The tail wheel stayed down all the time. But it was a reliable way to lower gear. I don't remember anyone coming in on their belly because the gear wouldn't go down. It was extremely forgiving, except for ground loops. And also extremely rugged. It had good armor plating and was beautifully put together. Grumman knew how to make tough planes. You couldn't pull the wings off it in a maneuver or anything like that.

The F4F was a ruggedly built aircraft capable of absorbing a good deal of punishment. This attribute saved the lives of many Naval Aviators in combat, with Wildcats routinely surviving being peppered by 7.7mm machine gun rounds fired by Zero-sens. F4Fs also endured frequent operational accidents landing back on the rough airfields synonymous with operations in the Solomons. This VF-11 Wildcat nosed over on Guadalcanal at the end of an eventful landing in July 1943. (127GR-3-61432, RG127, NARA)

CHAPTER 5
ART OF WAR

The primary mission of US Navy and US Marine Corps fighter squadrons was to protect aircraft, ships, and shore installations from enemy air attack. The secondary mission was to attack enemy aircraft, ships, and surface targets directly. F4F units flew CAPs over friendly forces, escorted strike aircraft on their missions, and carried out fighter sweeps and strafing attacks over enemy territory. Success came from employing correct tactics, effective teamwork and, above all, superior marksmanship, all of which were honed through hours, days, and months of practice.

The basic fighting team for both the US Navy and US Marine Corps fighter squadrons was the division of four aircraft, divided into two sections of two, with more experienced pilots leading the division and the section. During 1939–40, frontline fighter units had experimented with two-aircraft sections, rather than the traditional pre-war practice of using a section of three aircraft, with a leader and two wingmen. The US Navy duly adopted the two-aircraft section, and in July 1941 it ordered that fighter squadrons should be composed of three six-aircraft divisions, with each of the latter composed of three two-aircraft sections.

Experience in combat during 1942 would determine that a division of just two sections (totaling four aircraft) was superior, with pilots finding it easier to monitor each other's position and keep watch for enemy fighters. For Naval Aviators, the section was the building block for fighter tactics. Pilots were drilled to maneuver and fire as a unit, always striving to stick together at all times to survive in combat. Two aircraft could maneuver together, as could two sections and two or four divisions.

The basic tactic was to bracket enemy aircraft by placing individual aircraft, sections, or divisions above and on the bow of the enemy so that whichever way he turned, he would come under fire. Fighter pilots were instructed to strive to obtain superior altitude over enemy aircraft, and to keep together for mutual support, although this was not always possible if a combat broke down into a general melee. Above all else, US Navy fighter tactics and training stressed superiority of marksmanship. Naval Aviators assigned to fighter units were taught that their primary mission was to destroy enemy aircraft.

To a greater extent than in other air arms, the US Navy trained its pilots in gunnery approaches and deflection shooting. The basic premise was that when a fighter was in the correct position vis-à-vis an enemy aircraft, and its guns were properly aimed, the pilot would hit his target. The goal of the US Navy's gunnery training was to impart to its pilots a system for maneuvering their fighter into the correct position where proper aiming would result in the destruction of the enemy aircraft.

Instructors taught basic gunnery approaches from the side (high, flat, and low), from overhead, from head on, and from the rear. Aviation cadets began practicing these approaches during the advanced phase of their intermediate training, continued their practice at operational training units after earning their wings, and once they joined their squadrons, trained over and over until these approaches became second nature and could be flown instinctively.

Once in position to attack an enemy aircraft, the pilot had to aim correctly. The US Navy emphasized deflection shooting, teaching pilots how to lead an aircraft, firing ahead of the target so that the attacking fighter's bullets and the target would arrive at the same place at the same time. The pilot first had to determine where to aim. This depended on the speed of the enemy aircraft and its flight path. US Navy and US Marine Corps fighter pilots learned how to calculate an enemy aircraft's speed and range, and from this the amount of lead and firing angle, using the reticle on the Mk 8 Reflector Gunsight.

The next step was determining when to fire at the target. The US Navy recommended that the best range at which to open fire was from 1,000ft away from the enemy aircraft, closing to 200ft, and trained its pilots to use their gunsights to determine the distance to their target. As with gunnery approaches, deflection shooting had to be practiced over and over again until it, too, became second nature. As the US Navy's training materials noted, there was no time in the heat of combat for complex mathematical calculations. Pilots had to learn to determine the amount of lead and the correct point at which to open fire instantly.

The greatest challenge US Navy and US Marine Corps fighter pilots faced in the South Pacific was the Zero-sen. Its superiority over the Wildcat in climb, speed, and maneuverability came as a rude shock. Fortunately, in Lt Cdrs Jimmy Flatley and John Thach, the US Navy had two brilliant tacticians who worked out offensive and defensive tactics for defeating the Zero-sen in aerial combat.

As commander of VF-42, Flatley had fought the A6M during the Coral Sea battle, claiming one shot down and one damaged. Returning to America after the battle, Flatley reviewed his combats with the Zero-sen and those of his pilots, distilling these experiences into clear lessons. The central theme of

Lt Cdr James "Jimmy" Flatley was one of the US Navy's great fighter leaders and tacticians of World War II. From his experiences fighting with Zero-sens in the Coral Sea battle, Flatley developed tactics that Wildcat pilots could use to counter the IJNAF fighter's superior maneuverability, speed and rate of climb. (80G-398396, RG80, NARA)

the offensive tactics he developed was the recognition that Wildcat pilots were dealing with a fighter that was far more maneuverable, and attempting to follow a more maneuverable aircraft in combat would not work. In his Aircraft Action Report following his combat over the Coral Sea, Flatley explicitly made this point:

> The most effective attack against a more maneuverable fighter is to obtain altitude advantage, dive in, attack, and then pull up using speed gained in the dive to maintain altitude advantage. The old dogfight of chasing tails is not satisfactory and must not be employed when opposing Jap VF planes.

Flatley outlined an approach to dealing with the Zero-sen in his *Hints to Navy VF Pilots*, which were:

1. Gain plenty of altitude before contact with enemy VF [fighter]. You can lose altitude fast but you can't gain it fast enough when up against enemy VF.

2. Use hit-and-run attacks diving in and pulling out and up. If your target maneuvers out of your sight during your approach, pull out and let one of the following planes get him. If you attempt to twist and turn you will end up at his level or below, and will be unable to regain an altitude advantage. Following planes employ same tactics until you have destroyed the enemy one by one. Four planes is sufficient to carry out this attack. If you have others with you leave them overhead on guard.

3. If you get in a tough spot dive away, maneuver violently, find a cloud.

4. Stay together. The Japs' air discipline is excellent, and if you get separated you will have at least three of them on you at once.

5. You have the better airplane if you handle it properly, and in spite of their advantage of maneuverability, you can and should shoot them down with few losses to yourselves. The reason for this is your greater firepower and more skillful gunnery.

6. Don't get excited and rush in. Take your time and make the first attack effective.

7. Watch out for ruses. The Japs have a method of creating smoke from their exhaust which doesn't mean a thing. Set them on fire before you take your guns off them. They also have a method of releasing a gasoline cloud from their belly tanks.

8. Never hesitate to dive in. The hail of bullets around their cockpit will divert and confuse them and will definitely cause them to break-off what they are doing and take avoiding action.

Taking command of VF-10, Flatley incorporated these lessons into a manual – *Combat Doctrine: Fighting Squadron Ten* – for his new pilots. While preparing it, Flatley wrote a shorter letter titled "The Navy Fighter," laying out the key points of his offensive tactics and arguing in support of the F4F-4. These documents began to circulate among US Navy and US Marine Corps squadrons training for action in the South Pacific. Future high-scoring ace Capt Joe Foss, newly appointed executive officer of VMF-121, read a copy of Flatley's combat doctrine manual on his way across the Pacific.

Clearly there would be combats where the Zero-sen, and not the Wildcat, would have the advantage. Here, F4F pilots in the South Pacific benefited from Lt Cdr John Thach's work on defensive tactics against the A6M. Thach's tactics complemented Flatley's. Before the outbreak of war with Japan, Thach had been working on how the Wildcat could fight against a more maneuverable aircraft, particularly when attacked, based on intelligence reports he had read about the Zero-sen. He experimented using match sticks at his kitchen table and later with his pilots in VF-3.

Thach developed a defensive tactic against attack from above or behind in which two aircraft, or two sections of aircraft, flying abeam would turn toward each other when attacked and start weaving, continuing to turn toward each other until the attack was broken off. As the aircraft or sections turned toward each other, any attacking aircraft would immediately come under fire from the other aircraft or section. This maneuver, which came to be called the "Thach Weave," and later, officially, the Beam Defense Position, could also be used offensively. Thach's defensive tactic incorporated and reinforced the emphasis on coordinated teamwork that was also critically important in Flatley's offensive tactics. Flatley described the "Thach Weave" as "undoubtedly the greatest contribution to air combat tactics that has been made to date."

In early February 1943, an Allied air forces intelligence bulletin provided an account from Maj John Smith, CO of VMF-223, describing the tactics his squadron had used when engaging IJNAF bombers, and their Zero-sen escorts, over Guadalcanal. The unit had frequently employed Flatley's and Thach's tactics:

We always worked in pairs as much as possible. As a rule, the whole squadron would be used. Actually, there would be anywhere from 19 planes (that we landed on Guadalcanal with) down to five planes ready for flight operations. We always went together, and made the interception as a group.

We always climbed up in a very tight formation so that we would not get lost at high altitudes, as the Grumman had no excess power over 25,000ft.

Capt Joe Foss with members of his "flying circus" at Guadalcanal on January 4, 1943. They are, from left to right, 2Lt Roger Haberman (6.5 victories), 2Lt Cecil Doyle (five victories), Foss (26 victories), 1Lt Bill Marontate (12 victories), and 1Lt Roy Ruddell (three victories). Marontate was killed in action 11 days after this photograph was taken. (Tony Holmes Collection)

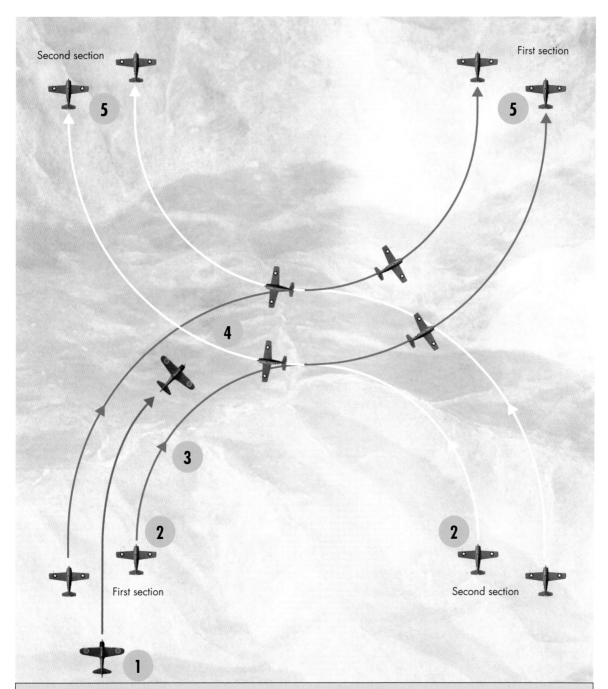

Second section

First section

5

5

4

3

2

2

First section

Second section

1

"THACH WEAVE" DIAGRAM

Lt Cdr John Thach developed this defensive tactic to counter the Zero-sen's superior maneuverability. When an IJNAF fighter (1) attacked a division of two sections (2) from the rear, the sections would turn sharply toward each other (3), giving the second section a head-on shot at the attacking Zero-sen (4). Dubbed the "Thach Weave" (5), and later officially called the Beam Defense Position, it became the standard defensive tactic for Naval Aviators against the Zero-sen.

If you weren't in formation, you were lost. We had the policy that if anybody lost a blower or the rubber gasket blew out of the auxiliary intake they would go to the east end of the island with the SBDs and circle around there until the air raid was over. It seemed to work all right, except that some pilots would get a little eager and if they could get to 18,000ft then they'd stay around over the combat area at that altitude waiting until one of the bombers got that low and then they would try to jump on him. That's the reason we lost some of the pilots we did, because they were too confident in their plane and themselves.

Groups of 26 were the enemy's favorite number, and they always had at least one Zeke [A6M] fighter with them for every bomber. At first, the Zekes stayed in four groups that we could see, one group above, one group below, and one group on either side. The Zeke pilots used no formation. They flew in a group of, say, five planes; and they did slow rolls and Immelmann turns, and all that sort of stuff, while they were flying along with the bombers, probably because they were a little faster than the bombers. It may sound foolish to you to say that they did slow rolls and Immelmanns while they were flying around there, and it seemed foolish to us, but actually that's what they did. I don't know why they did these aerobatics, unless it was possibly to look around better than they could while flying straight.

[After attacking the bombers] We'd pull back up again, and if the Zekes weren't there yet, we'd make another pass. The Jap bombers always flew a beautiful "V of V's" formation, with a 15-plane V and then the other 11 planes spaced in a V within that 15-plane V. I always tried to go across them from left to right, from their right to their left, in a straight line. And each pilot knew that if we went across them in that method, he was to take interval so that we could all make more or less simultaneous dives and yet not get in each other's way. I always took the left section, and the next man took the next one over and so on right down the line. And we always shot at the rear ones. That target had a width of about three-quarters of a mile. So you can see that we weren't all diving at any one point target. And I've seen as many as eight Grummans in a dive at one time, all shooting at a different airplane without any danger of collision.

The Jap bombers always flew in a three-plane formation in a "V

Lt Cdr John "Jimmy" Thach developed the defensive scheme that came to be known as the "Thach Weave" to counter the Zero-sen's superiority over the Wildcat. Successfully tested at Midway, US Navy and Marine Corps pilots employed the "Thach Weave" for the rest of the war. (80G-64822, RG80, NARA)

Aerial combat with the veteran pilots of IJNAF carrier- and land-based Zero-sen fighter units was a harsh school with little room for mistakes. Here, a US Marine Corps Wildcat lands back on Guadalcanal following an uneventful mission – the fabric covering the gun ports remains intact. (127GR-3-50898, RG127, NARA)

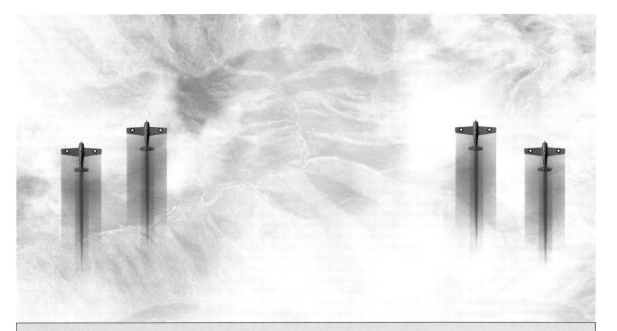

BEAM DEFENSE POSITION DIAGRAM

Lt Cdr John Thach's defensive weave maneuver was based on a division of two two-aircraft sections flying in what he called the Beam Defense Position in line abreast with a separation distance equal to the Wildcat's turning radius. The Beam Defense Position and the "Thach Weave" could be used either by both sections within a division of four aircraft (as illustrated here), or by single aircraft in a section of two fighters.

of V's". They never broke up formation. Their only evasive tactics were that as soon as they dropped their bomb, they'd nose down and pretend to lose altitude and gain speed as they went around the end of Florida Island and started home.

At one time (I think we all agreed on it pretty well), their indicated air speed at 20,000ft after they had dropped their bombs was about 150 knots because it took 12 to 15 minutes to get into position with the Grumman ("full gun" in high blower) to make an overhead pass on them. When there were no Zekes about, we did take all the time we wanted to get into position, and we always tried to drive home to the young pilots to shoot at the one plane and to shoot them down and then get out of there, and not try to spray the whole formation which looked like a beautiful target. You can see it would look very exciting to see a target three-quarters of a mile wide and big black bombers all over the place – the new pilots wanted to shoot them all down.

They did a lot of general shooting the first day, and didn't get any bombers at all. Then, they realized that you must stick to one enemy plane and shoot at him all the way down. Finally they did realize that if they did just that, they could see some results for their shooting. The Japs would catch on fire very readily; sometimes they'd even blow up. Sometimes, they'd just drop out of formation and slide down and go into the water.

There's a million incidents that we had that I won't mention, but that's the general method in fighting the Jap bombers. Always an overhead pass if you could get it – any high-side passes were at your own risk! I never made anything but overhead passes myself because that's all I consider is a decent gunnery pass with a ship with a 20mm stinger in it. And with the six guns the F4F has, you can easily open up 1,000ft above them and you can see obvious results of your shooting on the way down – if you hit them. The best pilots who knew a little bit about gunnery had better luck at first, but the others, as they came along, finally picked it up just as well as the older pilots.

A row of F4F-4s at "Fighter Two" on Guadalcanal in April 1943. During this period a number of US Marine Corps Wildcat squadrons in-theater were converting to the F4U, and the US Navy duly transferred several F4F-4 units, drawn from land bases and escort carriers, to augment the Corsair squadrons. (80G-41099)

CHAPTER 6
COMBAT

The intense aerial battles over Guadalcanal began on August 21, 1942 – the day after the first US Marine Corps Wildcat squadron had arrived on the island – and continued until mid-November, when Japanese air attacks began to taper off. From that period until April 1943, large clashes between F4F units and the enemy were less frequent, with Wildcat pilots making claims for ten or more Japanese aircraft on only five days. There were more regular smaller fights where the F4F squadrons encountered flights of Zero-sens and "Val" dive-bombers, claiming six or more shot down.

During June–July 1943 – the final months of the Wildcat's deployment in the South Pacific – US Navy F4F squadrons had some intense, hard-fought battles with Japanese fighters. In the early months the Japanese attacks followed a pattern that US Marine Corps and US Navy Wildcat pilots on Guadalcanal soon got used to. Maj Leonard K. Davis, who commanded VMF-121 on Guadalcanal until December 1942, and who claimed five Japanese aircraft shot down during his time on the island, recalled what a typical day was like:

Well, a typical day would usually be getting up at daybreak, going down to the mess hall, and getting whatever the boys had figured out to dish up. Which, with what they had, I think they did a good job. The first raid would normally be about ten o'clock in the morning. It almost became a clockwork routine. This ten o'clock so-called standby for the first raid would be augmented by coastwatcher reports through the Australian/New Zealand coastwatching network, which was a fantastic thing in getting the information out and not getting caught. Then one group of us would take off. We'd use all the available aircraft, which would seldom be more than 12 or 18, which meant that each pilot usually flew every other day as a rough go.

If the raid came down, we would do what we could to keep them from bombing and strafing and try and break it up before it got to the island, then come down, land and refuel. We ran out of gas once and had to sit on the ground for a couple

Capt Martin Clemens (rear center), an Australian coastwatcher on Guadalcanal, provided intelligence to Allied forces throughout the key months of action in the Solomons in 1942–43. The coastwatchers played a vitally important role when it came to alerting fighter units of approaching IJNAF bomber formations. The men with him were all members of the Solomon Islands police force. (Tony Holmes Collection)

of days because we were physically out of gas. We had even drained the B-17 bombers that were wrecks on the field and had some gas left in the tanks. We had gotten every bit of gas you could get.

Then there would usually be an afternoon raid at, maybe two or three o'clock, which we would go up to intercept. And then you'd usually have a couple of drinks. We had what we called a round table. And we'd have dinner and go back and have a couple of drinks. Well, you didn't have to worry about the guys getting loaded so they couldn't fly the next day because they were so tired that after one drink they'd be off to bed with the setting of the sun. This was something that everybody appreciated, to be able to have a bottle of beer.

Someone sent us up an Australian case of beer, which was a magnificent thing. It was 48 quarts. And it went over so well that I made arrangements through the transport pilots that were flying in MAG [Marine Air Group] 25 at that time to get two cases of beer a day into there. And despite the fact that the transports were loaded to the gunnels, the pilots said that they would cut down on their personal belongings and everything else in order to deliver this to us, and they did most regularly. They very seldom missed a day.

For new squadrons arriving on Guadalcanal there was a steep, but rapid, learning curve if pilots hoped to survive. As Davis recalled, "we profited from everything that had gone before. We made an effort to get our hands on anything that had been written or any oral observations or any lectures that we could get from returning pilots who had actually been in action. We took time out and made an effort to absorb all of that." But study was no substitute for experience; if a pilot survived the encounter, the lessons would never be forgotten, as 2Lt William Freeman and Capt Joe Foss found out.

An F4F-4 accelerating down the dirt runway at Henderson Field leaves a plume of dust in its wake. Taking off and landing safely, possibly in a damaged aircraft, was a constant challenge for Naval Aviators flying from airstrips on Guadalcanal. As this photograph clearly shows, operations in the Solomons in 1942–43 were "expeditionary" in US Marine Corps terminology. (Tony Holmes Collection)

Freeman was one of VMF-121's young pilots who had completed their training during 1942. In his case, Freeman had received his commission in March that year, then joined VMF-121 on its formation, before shipping out to the Pacific in September. On October 13, 1942, Freeman had his first encounter with Japanese aircraft, which was nearly his last, as he later recalled:

I became involved in air-to-air work for the first time due to a fluke. We scrambled at about 0930 in the morning, 1000 maybe, to intercept a raid which had been called in by a coastwatcher. We got a warning through the coastwatchers well in advance of the time it could be picked up by our radar, which was pretty short range. We took off, and my propeller pitch wouldn't change. The old Grumman had a Curtiss electric propeller, and there were times when those electric propellers, in the tropical humidity and environment and so on, simply would short out.

Anyway, I went grinding around the field, landed, and found another airplane that I could use and took off. The doctrine was, at that time, to climb to altitude over the field. I was now far behind the rest of the squadron, so I decided to take a course directly to where the raid was supposed to be coming in from. I figured that I would get there about the same time as my squadronmates, or perhaps a little later, but at least I would have a chance to take part in the interception. And I eventually got to a place that was about where the radar said the incoming aircraft were.

At that time I was flying at about 26,000ft, and when I looked down, directly coming at me, but 2,000ft below, were quite a number of Betty bombers. Well, I figured, "Okay, Bud, this is what you were trained for. Don't know where my friends are, but give it a shot." And I was dumb enough to try to get the guy in the middle rather than one of the guys on the end, because we'd heard a lot of propaganda that only the flight leaders really had good equipment and good bombsights and good crews. And if you got him, it usually broke up the raid. Well, I didn't take time to weigh up how valid this might be; I just didn't have time anyway.

So I turned over, and we were all trained in deflection shooting. So, I got the only overhead run that I ever got in World War II that time. Well, I got the middle guy. But it turned out that every waist gun and tail gun in 20-odd bombers had the opportunity to take a crack at me. Well, I didn't even hear anything, so after that guy started burning, I pulled up. I figured, "well, hell, this is what the book said you could do. And it was not quite that hard so I think I'll do it again."

As I started climbing up to get in position for another run, the airplane began to vibrate a little bit. I looked back, and there were at least three Zeros back there, seemingly taking turns trying to ventilate my posterior, and it seemed to me to be a very good idea to get out of there. The doctrine at that time in the old Grumman was to put the nose down straight, give it all the power you've got, roll to the right, and odds are they won't be able to follow you. It turned out they weren't.

I got back all right. And when I landed the airplane and taxied up, I noticed the groundcrew pointing at it and talking to each other. Well, I got it shut down and got out, and then I went back to see what they were pointing at. The fuselage was about half shot in two where the white star was, maybe three, four feet behind the cockpit. Nobody had enough lead. Anyhow, we all learned something from that one. When you start on a V of bombers, you take wingmen, not the middle guy.

On that same mission, Capt Joe Foss's exuberance at scoring his first aerial victory caused a lapse in attention that nearly cost him his life. Unaware that his radio was not working, Foss did not understand his wingman's frantic waving as a warning of Zero-sens above him. One IJNAF fighter dove down on Foss firing, but typically passed the F4F and pulled up ahead of him, giving Foss a clear shot. He fired, and saw the Zero-sen go down. Then, as he recounted in his autobiography *A Proud American*, all hell broke loose:

I felt charged with electricity – my hair standing on end and my mouth dry as cotton. I'd just gotten my first Zero. Straining against my lap belt to stand as erect as possible in the cramped cockpit, I yelled a victory war whoop at the top of my lungs.

Busy celebrating, I failed to see the three Zeros lining up on me – until I found myself in the midst of streaming tracers. "Got to head out of here, fast!" I said aloud. I jammed the stick forward and went into a screaming dive from 22,000ft. I'd read that a Zero couldn't follow such a dive; its wings would come off trying to pull out. Well, whoever wrote that was a fiction writer, because those boys just kept on my tail, pumping lead! Two shells entered my fuselage. Dark smokey oil spewed out the right oil cooler. With its lubrication pouring into the air, the high-speed engine froze almost instantly. Clouds of smoke replaced oil, pierced by tracers from the three planes on my tail.

When the engine seized, the reduction gear between the propeller and the engine was wrenched off and the prop became a free agent, causing extreme vibrations. Between the wind shrieking through the holes in the canopy and the rotating prop with its ruined connections, the noise level was deafening. And if that wasn't enough to get my attention, through the side of the canopy I stared wide-eyed at a gaping hole in my wing where a 20mm cannon shell had exploded. I could see the ocean through it.

Henderson Field in September 1942, with Wildcats on the field and the 1st Marine Air Wing's air operations center in the background, dubbed "The Pagoda". It was destroyed in a Japanese air raid in October. (80G-20673, RG80, NARA)

In an almost vertical dive, picking up airspeed rapidly, violent vibrations set in. When the earth took up most of my field of vision, I pulled back on the stick with all my strength, hoping the tail assembly was still functional, and leveled out just over the ground. Streaking dead stick just above the trees, I headed for the field, at the same time worrying about keeping as much distance as possible between myself and the closing Zeros.

By now I was only 150ft off the ground, my pursuers hot on me, still sending sizzling streamers in my direction. I was coming in much too fast – 150 knots, when 90 was considered the maximum for a safe landing – but if I slowed down they'd blast me out of the sky. The piercing, penetrating racket increased, the vibrations were unbelievable. The vacuum flaps designed to slow the plane refused to deploy at 150 knots. Only the landing gear that I had dropped was slowing me down. In a desperate attempt to line up the runway, I sideslipped the Wildcat. It set down, hitting hard, but keeping upright. I managed to turn 45 degrees into the palm grove and was fortunate enough to go bumping down the only row between the palm trees that was clear of barrels or trenches. When I finally came to a stop, I just sat there thinking, "The score is tied – I'm ready to be a farmer again".

That day Foss learned an indelible lesson: to stay alive, a pilot had to stay alert at all times, constantly scanning for enemy fighters. He practiced his new lesson so much that he said his squadronmates took to calling him "Swivel-neck Joe".

It was not just the inexperienced pilots who ran afoul of the Zero-sens escorting the bombers to Henderson Field. On September 9, 1942, Capt Marion Carl led eight F4Fs from VMF-223 to intercept an incoming raid of 26 "Betty" bombers with an escort of some 20 Zero-sens. By a bizarre coincidence, this happened to be Carl's 13th mission from Guadalcanal, and he was flying his regular F4F, No. 13. Carl made two passes at the bomber formation, and claimed two destroyed, the second of which was his 13th victory, but instead of diving away and heading for the clouds, he decided to go in for a third pass.

As Carl approached the bombers, an unseen IJNAF fighter riddled his Wildcat with 20mm cannon shells. "A Zero hit me with 20mm cannon," he told the press upon returning home in early 1943, "How many times I do not know. I was at 22,000ft when my plane burst into flames. I lost no time bailing out and landed in the water several miles from Guadalcanal and 30 miles down the coast from Henderson Field." Carl survived his bailout and dunking in the sea, and with the help of local islanders made his way back to Henderson a few days later.

By early September 1942, the near daily air raids and operational accidents had been a steady drain on the aircraft available to VMF-223 and its sister squadron, VMF-224, which had arrived on Guadalcanal on August 30.

0930 hrs, SEPTEMBER 13, 1942

GUADALCANAL, SOLOMON ISLANDS

1 After being scrambled from Henderson Field, Lt Walter E. Clarke of VF-5 leads his division in two loose two-aircraft sections for altitude, with Ens Mortimer C. Kleinmann as his wingman, and Lt(jg) Elisha T. "Smoky" Stover leading Ens Donald A. Innis as the second section. Note that the aircraft numbers worn by the Wildcats in all of the diagrams within this book are representative, and not the actual numbers of the aircraft participating in the missions depicted in artwork. US Navy and US Marine Corps pilots typically recorded the unique Bureau of Aeronautics number of the aircraft they flew, but not the fighter's individual single or two-digit fuselage/tail number.

2 As the Wildcat pilots reach 25,000ft, six A6M2 Zero-sens from the Tainan Kokutai jump the division, quickly setting Ens Innis' Wildcat on fire. Innis bails out immediately, his fighter falling in flames.

3 Clarke and Stover follow Innis down, circling, till they reach 12,000ft, where three Zero-sens jump them.

4 One Zero-sen riddles Stover's tail.

5 Stover dives down to 8,000ft, with a Zero-sen following him. When the IJNAF fighter pulls up in front of him, Stover fires a short burst and sees the enemy aircraft go down in flames.

6 Clarke also has to dive into the clouds to dodge attacking Zero-sens. Coming out of a cloud, he spots one of the A6M2s performing a wingover and fires, causing the fighter to burst into flames.

7 Two more Zero-sens attack Stover, forcing him to also seek cover in the clouds for 30 minutes. He dodges in and out of the clouds, with the two enemy fighters above him making passes at his Wildcat whenever he emerges from cover.

8 After 30 minutes the Zero-sens give up the chase.

9 Stover and Clarke disengage from the enemy and head back to Henderson Field, the former landing without flaps due to damage to his wings.

FOLLOWING PAGES

Between August 24 and September 9, the two units had lost 27 aircraft in combat, from bombing and through accidents. The poor condition of Henderson Field led to five aircraft being lost on September 8, one on take-off and four returning from a scramble after dark. Forty-eight hours later, there were just 11 flyable F4Fs at Henderson Field.

To quickly reinforce the US Marine Corps Wildcat squadrons of the Cactus Air Force, Rear Adm John McCain, Commander, Aircraft, South Pacific Force, ordered the US Navy's VF-5, temporarily ashore at Efate, on Vanuatu, to fly its 24 F4Fs to Guadalcanal. Lt Cdr Leroy Simpler duly led his squadron to the island on September 11.

Two young Wildcat pilots who made their first claims over Guadalcanal with VF-5 were Lt(jg) Elisha T. "Smokey" Stover and Ens John Wesolowski. Stover had completed his training in July 1941, after which he was assigned to VF-8 embarked in USS *Hornet* (CV-8) and participated in the Battle of Midway. Following the latter, he was promoted to lieutenant (junior grade) and assigned to VF-5. Wesolowski had received his wings of gold in October 1941 and went directly to VF-5.

Having completed their training during 1941, Wesolowski and Stover were part of the group of younger pilots who had close to 600 hours of flying time in their logbooks prior to seeing combat. They both flew during the Battle of the Eastern Solomons, but neither made a claim for a Japanese aircraft.

Wesolowski was the first to score, claiming a "Betty" shot down on September 12, 1942, during VF-5's first combat action from Guadalcanal. Twenty Wildcats from the unit had joined ten US Marine Corps F4Fs led by now-Maj John Smith in the interception of an incoming raid of 26 Type 1 bombers with an escort of 15 Zero-sens. Wesolowski was flying as wingman for Lt Walter Clarke. With other VF-5 divisions taking on the escort, Clarke led his division in an attack on the bombers, which had already been targeted by Smith's Wildcats. Lagging behind Clarke, Wesolowski fired on a straggling Type 1 that Smith and Clarke had already damaged, sending the bomber down into the sea near Savo Island after firing off 1,000 rounds of his ammunition. Wesolowski's comments in his Aircraft Action Report were brief:

> Failed to intercept before they dropped bombs. They came in at 24,000ft, escorted by "Zero" fighters below and behind them. We failed to get altitude and position in time after notification of raid. Enemy VB [bombers], about 26 in number, pushed over in a shallow dive to 21,000ft, dropped bombs over Henderson Field, turned northwest toward Savo Island, and we chased them to Savo, where we were able to reach them and attack. I succeeded in shooting one of them down. One "Zero" attempted to attack me but without success.

Two days later, Wesolowski participated in the late interception of a raid by 19 F1M2 Type 0 Observation ("Pete") seaplanes attempting to bomb Henderson Field. Separated from the rest of VF-5, Wesolowski found eight "Petes" north of Savo Island in the fading evening light. He attacked the trailing aircraft in the formation, and believing he had set it on fire, he pulled up behind the leader and engaged it until he again saw what he thought were flames streaming from his quarry. Wesolowski broke off his attack to return to Henderson while

46

FIGHTING FIVE

there was still light, claiming two of the seaplanes destroyed. In fact, he had managed to damage only one of the aircraft, which made it back to base.

Wesolowski did not claim again until September 27, when he was fortunate to survive an encounter with Zero-sens as he struggled to join the rest of VF-5 as it climbed to intercept an incoming raid. Years later, he gave an account of this incident to Eric Hammel for his volume *Aces Against Japan – The American Aces Speak*:

Shortly after 1300 on September 27, 1942, we were alerted and scrambled as usual. Marine F4Fs from VMF-223 and VMF-224 also took off. I was the wingman of my squadron commander, Lt Cdr Leroy Simpler, and I joined up on him. Behind me was our second section and a couple of other four-plane divisions of the squadron. The skipper then proceeded to climb at maximum power, but my plane and several others simply couldn't keep up, even at full power. Believe me, we had the best mechanics in the world, working in almost unbelievable conditions, but some planes just did not perform as well as others. Spark plug age might have had an effect because we weren't able to perform the routine 30-hour checks on the

US Navy fighter squadron VF-5 joined the US Marine Corps Wildcat units on Guadalcanal in September 1942, and this group photograph shows its pilot cadre on the island toward the end of that same month. Bearded Ens John Wesolowski is standing in the back row, fifth from the left, while Lt(jg) "Smokey" Stover is in the same row, second from the right. (80-40809, RG80, NARA)

planes and were scavenging parts from here and there. No doubt, Lt Cdr Simpler's plane was better tended to than many of the others.

Eventually, I lost sight of the skipper and the rest of the squadron in the clouds, but I knew their altitude and general location by way of my radio, so I kept trying to catch up. There were other stragglers, and we stragglers were loosely joined a few thousand feet below and behind the main body of the squadron. I soon got ahead of the other stragglers and lost sight of them, too. I was completely alone.

When I was somewhere in the neighborhood of 21,000ft in an all-out climb at about 105 knots airspeed, I swear I heard machine gun fire. I looked back in my rearview mirror and saw two Zekes diving on me and firing. Of course, it is not possible to hear machine guns in those circumstances, but I thought I did. More likely, I felt bullets impacting on my plane. By the time I looked back, the two Zekes had already flattened out from their high-side pass on me and were essentially at my altitude. They were both firing; I could see the muzzle flashes.

I immediately nosed over to get some airspeed and, when I did, I saw a third Zeke. I believe he overshot me while making a pass on me. When I saw him, he was below, ahead and pretty close. He was in the process of pulling up, probably to get a new altitude advantage. He was dead in front of me and in my sights, so I fired at him – almost reflexively. My pipper must have been at least 50 mils or so in front of him because he was starting up and I was starting down. This was really a snap shot from someone whose main purpose was to get out of a nasty situation. I had all six of my guns charged and the ammo mix was one tracer every fourth round in each gun. We also had a mix of standard and armor-piercing ammo. I can't say how long a burst I fired, but I think it was quite short. I don't know where I hit him; he just seemed to break apart with little or no fire associated. He was only there for an instant; I may have overshot him before smoke and flames occurred.

I was thinking of the two Zekes that were still on my tail, so I continued to nose down almost vertically. As my speed went up, I did an aileron roll onto my back and started to pull through. That is, I dove away vertically and then, as the speed built up, executed what amounted to a half slow roll, except I was vertical. When my orientation was 180 degrees from where I had started, I intended to pull out as fast as I could so that my ending direction was the reverse of my starting heading.

We had often discussed doing this evasive maneuver; we felt that the Zero was not rugged enough to follow it without suffering structural damage. However, I was having a pretty difficult time myself. I couldn't seem to pull out because I was going so fast by then. I don't know what the airspeed was since the needle was on its third time around the dial, which was only calibrated for two turns. I was reluctant to use the trim tab for fear of pulling too many Gs and breaking up my own plane. I also discarded the idea of bailing out, because I knew that as soon as I opened the canopy the airstream would probably tear the plane apart. So I kept pulling back on the stick and very slowly got my fighter under control. I had long since lost track of the two Zekes.

When I finally got pulled out at about 600ft, I was going way over 400 knots. I then started to climb back up to join the squadron, whose chatter I could hear over the radio. By the time I got to 16,000ft, however, the squadron had been ordered back to base, so I followed it in.

Wesolowski's final claim on Guadalcanal came on September 28, when Wildcat pilots severely punished attacking Type 1 bombers, claiming 23 out of 25 shot down. In fact, the F4F units had shot down five bombers between them, with two more crash-landing, a third having to be scrapped and the surviving 17 all damaged to varying degrees. Wesolowski was flying in Lt Howard Crews' division, with Crews leading 11 VF-5 aircraft in an attack on the bomber formation shortly after Smith's VMF-223 had engaged the "Bettys."

Wesolowski's was the last Wildcat in his division to attack, making a high-side run on one of the bombers. He saw two going down in flames as he pulled in on his target and fired, hitting the bomber's left wing root and causing it to burn. Wesolowski then dove down to 12,000ft, where he joined two US Marine Corps Wildcats. His last sight of the bomber formation was of six aircraft withdrawing, with two smoking badly and still coming under attack. Later promoted to lieutenant, Wesolowski participated in the Okinawa campaign with F6F-5 Hellcat-equipped VBF-9, claiming two more Japanese aircraft shot down.

"Smokey" Stover missed VF-5's first combat mission on September 12 when his F4F failed to start, but he claimed a Zero-sen shot down and a second one as a probable the next day. That morning the IJNAF had sent a reconnaissance aircraft to Guadalcanal with an escort of nine Tainan Kokutai Zero-sens. When Henderson Field radar detected bogies coming in, Lt Clarke scrambled with his division to join other VF-5 and VMF-224 Wildcats patrolling at high altitude. Climbing hard to intercept the enemy aircraft, Clarke's wingman suffered a blown gasket in his supercharger and had to dive away. Clarke continued climbing, with Stover behind him and Lt(jg) Don Innis following.

Seeing the Wildcats below them, six Zero-sens broke off and bounced Clarke and his wingmen when they had reached 25,000ft, setting Innis' F4F on fire and forcing him to bail out. Clarke and Stover dove away, with the enemy fighters following, as Stover noted in his Aircraft Action Report:

One "Zero" riddled my tail. I dove out and down to 8,000ft. One of them followed and pulled up in front. I gave him one short burst and he went down in flames. I saw him burning on the hilltop. Immediately after I gave another one a burst. He put out white smoke and made two complete circles, after which I was unable to observe results because of renewed attacks.

I went into clouds then, and stayed there for 30 minutes, dodging in and out, while two "Zeros" remained 1,000ft above clouds, making passes on me whenever I came out. After 30 minutes they left, and I climbed to altitude to test my damaged plane and then returned to base. They had hit my rudder and stabilizer, leaving the rudder riddled and tab control damaged. The vacuum tank was also riddled. There was a large hole in one wing trailing edge that prevented use of flaps. Tail wheel locking severed. Armor plate very good.

In his battle with the Zero-sens Stover had used up nearly all of his ammunition. Despite the extensive damage to his Wildcat, he commented that the Japanese pilots showed poor gunnery.

When VF-5 fought "Pete" seaplanes and their escorting A6M2-N Type 2 ("Rufe") floatplane fighters on September 14, Stover claimed one example of each type destroyed. Two weeks later, he had an inconclusive combat with a Zero-sen, and his final claim came on October 15 – the day before VF-5 left Guadalcanal. That morning, Lt Carl Rooney and Stover went out on a mission to strafe six Japanese transports off Guadalcanal. Diving down from 7,000ft, Rooney and Stover strafed three transports in line, seeing hits, and running the gauntlet of anti-aircraft fire from escorting IJN destroyers nearby. Completing their first run, they flew over the island and climbed for altitude to begin their second run. Pulling up from this run, Stover was above the transports at an altitude of 7,000ft when he saw a Type 0 Observation seaplane diving down to attack him:

After [I] pulled out of the second run, [I] noted a seaplane coming down from the rear when we were at 7,000ft. I turned at right angles to his course and started climbing. He started climbing also. I was not gaining altitude on him at 8,000ft, so I turned toward him and we approached each other for at least half a mile. He opened fire at extremely long range with two synchronized guns, possibly 20mm. His fire dribbled off to my right. I opened fire at 500 yards but was unable to observe any effect. Only four of my six guns were firing.

We both continued in our head-on runs and delayed pull out so long that we crashed in mid-air, my right wing hitting both of his right wings. Finding that my plane was still controllable, I turned and saw the Jap plane below me, apparently having trouble. I made another run and only one gun fired. I doubt whether I got a hit on that run. I observed the Jap go off in a spin, and Lt Rooney reported that he crashed. I was too busy with my own troubles to observe the final effect on the Jap. I proceeded to Henderson Field and landed. I found pieces of fabric (including a rising sun) on the leading edge of my plane.

October 1942 was a month of crisis on Guadalcanal, with the Japanese making a determined effort to deny the Americans possession of the island. This F4F was destroyed during an IJNAF bombing raid on Henderson Field, the aircraft appearing to have suffered a direct hit from ordnance dropped by a "Betty" bomber. (US Marine Corps 61548/ NARA)

On landing, Stover found a large gash in the leading edge of his right wing that contained the fabric torn from the Type O Observation seaplane's upper wing. His right flap had been partially torn off and bent down, and there were four large holes in his fuselage that he had picked up strafing the Japanese transports. Returning home, Stover was promoted to lieutenant and served in the Combat Information Center on board the new USS *Yorktown* (CV-10). At his request, Stover went back to combat flying, rejoining Hellcat-equipped VF-5 in early 1944, only to be killed in action during the February 17 attack on Truk.

October 1942 was the most difficult month in the battle for Guadalcanal, the situation on the ground, at sea, and in the air reaching the point of crisis. The Japanese were determined to recapture the island, bringing in more troops, supplies, and naval vessels to shell Henderson Field and the newly built "Fighter One" airstrip by night. The IJNAF reinforced its units at Rabaul and prepared bases for bombers at Buka, on the northern tip of Bougainville, and for fighters at Buin, at the southern tip of the island, shortening the range to Guadalcanal.

On Guadalcanal, MAG-14 replaced the depleted MAG-23, bringing in VMF-121 and VMF-212 in the middle of the month to replace VMF-223 and VMF-224. The new squadrons would take their early combat lessons to heart, and after just two weeks on the island they had claimed some 120 Japanese aircraft shot down.

On October 26 came the Battle of Santa Cruz, where Japanese and American carriers met in battle once more and the IJN emerged victorious following the destruction of *Hornet*, leaving *Enterprise* as the only surviving US Navy carrier in the South Pacific – *Wasp* having been torpedoed and sunk on September 15.

During October, Allied air units in the South Pacific claimed 370 Japanese aircraft destroyed – more than in any other month between August and December 1942 – such was the intensity of air combat.

Pilots from VMF-212 pose for a photograph on Espiritu Santo prior to transferring to Guadalcanal on October 16, 1942. The squadron's CO, Lt Col "Joe" Bauer, is standing seventh from the left, behind the wooden panel adorned with the squadron's insignia. Bauer had helped to establish this unit on March 1, 1942, and the majority of the pilots under his command were young second lieutenants with only a few hundred hours of flying experience. Nevertheless, by the time VMF-212 fought its final combat with the IJNAF over Guadalcanal in mid-November, these men had claimed 57 victories between them. (80G-357147, RG80, NARA)

Between October 18–25, the IJNAF carried out five raids on Guadalcanal in an attempt to knock out Henderson Field, although with fewer bombers on each mission than had been the case in August and September. On three days, in the swirling combats, US Marine Corps and USAAF pilots claimed more than 20 enemy aircraft shot down, although the actual Japanese losses were no doubt lower. In his wartime volume *Joe Foss – Flying Marine*, written with Walter Simmons and intended to inspire a domestic American audience, Foss described the intense combat of October 23, when he claimed four Zero-sens shot down. His account contained appropriate hyperbole for the time period:

> The first thing I knew a Grumman came across my course at an angle, pouring lead into a Zero that was trying to get away. On the Wildcat's tail another Zero was hanging, pumping away with machine guns and cannon. I swung in behind this Zero. When I was only a few feet away, I gave it to him. Poof! He blew up and disintegrated. I swung over hard to miss the falling junk.
>
> The sky was filled with wild dogfights. I got on to the tail of a Jap, but he saw me coming and went into a dive. Then he pulled out and went into a loop. I cut close inside, and as he went over on his back, I thought, "hell, this is the thing I've been waiting for." I was upside down when I led him with a good spray from my six 0.50-cal. machine guns. The fire converged in a lucky shot. He blew up in a great, beautiful burst, and I ducked as the Grumman went through the pieces.
>
> I was conscious of explosions, fires, and streams of tracers on all sides. The dogfight wound up tight in a small area, and the sky was filled with death. I came

Capt Joe Foss reunited with veterans of VMF-121 in the US following their return home. All were entitled to wear combat and campaign ribbons, but none did so on this occasion. In the front row, from left to right, are 2Lts Robert Haberman (6.5 victories) and Frank Presley (4.5 victories), while standing in the rear, again from left to right, are 2Lt Oscar Bate (five victories), Capt Greg Loesch (8.5 victories), Foss (26 victories), and 2Lts Bill Freeman (six victories) and Thomas "Boot" Furlow (three victories). (Tony Holmes Collection)

out of the loop and put my nose down to gain speed. Out of nowhere came a maniac in a Zero, going up at an angle and breaking into a slow roll. He must have thought he had got somebody and was due for a celebration. When he was three-quarters around, I pulled up and gave him a quick squirt. There was a lovely, blinding flash, and the pilot popped out, nearly hitting my Grumman. I barely managed to hop over him as he plummeted down toward the island and the sea, both looking so incredibly peaceful below.

But this was no spot for a nature lover. Leveling out of a dive, two Zeros were coming for me – one head-on, the other from an angle. I made for the first one. While I was wondering if he intended to ram me, he pulled up to his right. I got in a short burst back of his motor, and flames were lapping at him as I went by. He blew up when right off my left wing.

Foss was fortunate that he did not have to pay dearly for his exuberance. In his last attack the Zero-sen making a head-on approach hit his engine, which started smoking just as another Zero-sen attacked him from behind. Diving away, the fighter followed him, but overran Foss just as another Zero-sen made a firing pass at his Wildcat. Foss called for help, and two fellow Wildcat pilots chased off the Zero-sens, allowing him to bring his damaged Grumman back to the field. Two days later he would claim another four Zero-sens.

Three days after Foss's combat, the Battle of Santa Cruz took place in the waters to the east of the Solomon Islands. This clash between IJN and US Navy carriers has been covered in detail in several books, notably John Lundstrom's *The First Team and the Guadalcanal Campaign*. The IJN's Combined Fleet went into battle with the fleet carriers *Shokaku* and *Zuikaku* and the light carrier *Zuiho* ranged against the US Navy's *Enterprise* and *Hornet*.

On the morning of October 26, IJNAF and US Navy strike groups went after each other's carriers, the Americans damaging *Shokaku* and *Zuiho* and the Japanese fatally hitting *Hornet*. Flying as escort to the strike groups and in CAPs in defense of their carriers, the Wildcat pilots of VF-10 embarked in *Enterprise* and VF-72 on board *Hornet* claimed 66 enemy aircraft shot down, with a further 27 probably shot down. Lundstrom has estimated that the IJNAF carrier units lost 16 "Vals," ten "Kates," and three Zero-sens to the Wildcat squadrons, with an additional 25 aircraft shot down by American anti-aircraft fire.

That morning, VF-10 pilots, and future aces, Ens Edward Feightner and Ens Donald Gordon had their first combats with Japanese aircraft. Flying with Ens Maurice Wickendoll on CAP, Feightner claimed a "Val" shot down and a "Kate" as a probable. Gordon, who left a detailed Aircraft Action Report of his combats on October 26, was credited with two "Kates" destroyed and a third as a probable:

At 0930, October 26, 1942, I took off from the USS ENTERPRISE for CAP. As I took off, it was announced over radio that enemy planes were coming in from the northwest. The first plane off proceeded to start a spiral climb over the ship. I was the fourth plane off, so I followed the other three, and other planes were following behind me. At 7,000ft, Ens Davis [Gerald V. Davis] joined up on me and we proceeded to climb up to 15,000ft.

The Battle of Santa Cruz – the second, and final, clash between IJN and US Navy carriers until the Battle of the Philippine Sea in June 1944 – took place on October 26, 1942. Here, deck crew manually unfold the starboard wing of an F4F-4 from VF-10 as it is prepared for take-off from *Enterprise*. (80G-30005, RG80, NARA)

During the time we were climbing, we went in the direction of the USS HORNET, which was west of the ENTERPRISE. When we got to 15,000ft, we were on a bearing of about 230° (T) from the HORNET, distance five miles. At this time, a "Tally-Ho" was made on some torpedo planes which were at 7,000ft. Looking down, they were directly beneath us. I picked out a lone plane about a mile south of the rest. I turned on my gun switches and started down, Ens Davis with me. I came in flat, for he was close to the [anti-aircraft fire] screen by this time. I opened fire with my sights on, but had so much speed, my bullets went over. He didn't know we were there until I opened fire. Then he made a right turn, which was just right for Ens Davis, who was flying under my starboard wing. He opened fire as I pulled away, and followed the plane. I turned back and joined him after he pulled out. His fire caused the plane to smoke and the plane turned away from the fleet.

Instead of following it, we jumped another that was going in, and again I missed my first pass, but I did make him smoke. His rear gun didn't work on the first pass, so the next pass I came right on in and he exploded about ten feet off the water. At this time, there was a plane burning at the place where we attacked the other planes. It is very possible that Ens Davis did get him, for it was black smoke and not the white smoke they use.

That was all the action I was in over the HORNET. [Wildcat] F-10 of the HORNET had joined us, and he headed for the ENTERPRISE to refuel and arm. Ens Davis and I started to climb, but he had motor trouble and we came back to land. I'm sure he wasn't hit for I never saw anything come at us. We broke off and got in the landing circle. An attack came in over the ENTERPRISE while I was around the ship. I rolled up my wheels and started to climb. I didn't see anybody to join, so I went by myself.

At 10,000ft, two dive-bombers went in in front of me. I fired at both, but missed, so I started to climb out of the AA [anti-aircraft fire] when I met another dive-bomber and fired at him and all my guns quit and he started to smoke. I was out of ammunition. I watched him pull out at about 4,000ft and he exploded. I might have gotten him, but AA probably did. Being out of ammunition, I came back down to the water and joined on Ens Reding [Willis B. Reding]. His guns wouldn't work, so we hung together and later were joined by two VF-8 pilots.

When the torpedo attack came in, we were all south of the ship by five miles. As we circled, two torpedo planes came out toward us. We were at about 500ft and they were at about ten feet. One of the VF-8 pilots dived at one, so I dived at the other, hoping against hope that my guns might work. They didn't. The little Jap must have looked up all of a sudden and, seeing me, turned his plane, and in doing so caught his wing in the water and burned up.

Future ace Ens Donald "Flash" Gordon flew with VF-10 during the Santa Cruz battle, claiming two Type 97 Carrier Bombers shot down and a third as a probable in his first encounter with Japanese aircraft. (80G-39603, RG80, NARA)

During the next attack, I stayed in the clouds with somebody else. I never was scared until I had been on my reserve for 45 minutes and then got a wave-off. It is possible Ens Davis got shot down by his own AA in the landing circle, for these boys didn't care who they shot at.

I broke every rule in the book by being by myself and then running out of ammunition without doing anything. I just held the trigger. I hope I know more and do better next time. I learned an awful lot.

Gordon did learn from this experience, going on to claim another Type 1 bomber on January 30, 1943, and after VF-10 re-equipped with the F6F Hellcat, being credited with four more Japanese aircraft shot down during 1944. Ens Davis disappeared during the battle, possibly shot down by the fleet's anti-aircraft fire, as Gordon suspected, or possibly having fallen victim to a Zero-sen.

Following the raids of late October and the Battle of Santa Cruz, there was a lull in the air war over Guadalcanal. The US Marine Corps Wildcat squadrons received reinforcements when VMF-112 arrived in early November. The air battle resumed on November 11 when nine "Vals" with 18 escorting Zero-sens attacked American shipping off-loading supplies for Guadalcanal's defenders. US Marine Corps F4F pilots claimed four of the dive-bombers and two Zero-sens shot down, but no fewer than six Wildcats and four pilots were lost in return. A later attack on Henderson Field that same day resulted in four "Betty" bombers being shot down, although two more F4Fs were destroyed in a mid-air collision during the engagement.

The next day, 16 torpedo-armed "Bettys" escorted by 30 Zero-sens made another attack on American shipping, with disastrous results. Wildcats from VMF-121 and the newly arrived VMF-112, plus USAAF P-39s, took off to intercept the incoming raiders. In the combats that ensued, the IJNAF lost 11 "Bettys" and a single Zero-sen. The surviving bombers received so much damage that they too were written off upon returning to base.

Amongst the young second lieutenants flying that day was Jefferson DeBlanc, on only his second combat mission. He was one of seven VMF-112 pilots who scrambled in the early afternoon against the Japanese raiding force, flying as wingman to Lt James Secrest. As the Wildcats reached 5,000ft, squadron CO Maj Paul Fontana drew their attention to anti-aircraft fire coming up from the ships below them. DeBlanc described getting his first two claims in his memoir, *The Guadalcanal Air War – Col. Jefferson DeBlanc's Story*:

In early November 1942, VMF-112 arrived on Guadalcanal from Nouméa. One of the young aviators in the squadron was 2Lt Jefferson DeBlanc, who went into combat with fewer than the normal 40 hours of flying time considered necessary for a pilot to become familiar with the Wildcat. Unfazed by this, DeBlanc claimed two "Betty" bombers shot down on November 12 on only his second combat mission. On January 31 he would claim five aircraft destroyed while defending US Marine Corps SBDs. The latter feat earned DeBlanc the Medal of Honor. (DM-SD-03-09572, NARA)

Looking down at the fleet, I saw 15 or more twin-engined Betty torpedo-bombers coming around the 'Canal and starting a high-speed run on the fleet at about 50ft. They were in the most perfectly strung-out run I have ever seen, and this time we had the advantage. It was a fighter pilot's dream. The altitude was ours, and we would not have to compensate for speed and position – just dive on the sitting ducks below us. Under no circumstances would I ever be a bomber pilot in combat! Our fleet was at a disadvantage. They could not maneuver to avoid the bombers, and had difficulty lowering the deck guns from the "up" position to the "down" position at the waterline for firing purposes. Regardless, they were sending up a huge barrage of anti-aircraft fire that we had to fly through.

Joe Foss and his flight had spotted the Japanese bombers and were on the way down from 25,000ft to engage them. My flight dived through the AA fire, and two of our fighters were hit and crashed into the ocean. Then we hit the enemy bombers at high speed. The action was too fast and fierce for fear to catch up with me. I flew through the barrage from the fleet and locked on to the tail of a Betty and opened fire, killing the rear gunner and watching my tracers strike the engines. The plane burst into flames immediately, and I almost flew into the bomber due to target fixation. I was awed by the winding down of its two engines' propellers as seen through my own propeller turning at greater revolutions. The stroboscopic effect was hypnotic. Flying through the heat generated by the flaming bomber, I quickly recovered and locked on to the tail of another bomber adjacent to me at about 50ft off the water. I sent this one crashing in flames with a short burst of the six 0.50-cal. machine guns.

I had cleared the fleet by this time, knowing that there were other bombers coming out of their runs and clearing the fleet as well. A wingover placed my fighter back in the action 50ft over the water. Sure enough, there was a last bomber clearing the run and starting for home. With a little motion of the rudder and stick, I lined up with the Wildcat for a head-on run, coming down on him from a little above his flight path. It didn't take long to bring the bomber fully within the rings of the projected gunsight on my windshield. I locked on fast, and quickly let go a short, deadly burst of machine gun fire. The burst caught the left engine and smoked it as my tracers also hit and shattered the pilot greenhouse area.

Two-and-a-half months after this combat, on January 31, 1943, DeBlanc would claim two Type 0 Observation seaplanes and three Zero-sens shot down over Vella Gulf while protecting a flight of SBD dive-bombers – an "ace in a day" feat that earned him the Medal of Honor.

The IJN attempted to destroy Henderson Field and the two nearby fighter airstrips through bombardment on the night of November 13, and it tried again the following night, leading to the Naval Battle of Guadalcanal that saw US Navy vessels engage enemy warships. The Americans would lose two light cruisers and seven destroyers in the battle, but Henderson Field survived.

During daylight hours on November 14, US Marine Corps and US Navy torpedo- and dive-bombers attacked a Japanese convoy bringing reinforcements for Guadalcanal, sinking seven out of 11 transports and claiming 21 Zero-sens and Type 0 Observation seaplanes shot down. This proved to be the last major engagement fought by US Marine Corps Wildcats for nearly two months. Although the Japanese did not decide to withdraw from Guadalcanal until the end of 1942, they never again made a significant effort to take back the island.

With the hiatus in enemy air attacks, reinforcements arrived on Guadalcanal in the form of US Army infantry and US Marine Corps divisions, and more aircraft, including the first squadron of USAAF P-38 Lightnings. By the end of November, MAG-14 had 71 F4F-4s on the island. The air campaign now shifted to stopping IJN shipping coming down the "Slot" with supplies for

MEDAL OF HONOR ACTION

At 1500 hrs on January 31, 1943, VMF-112 sent off two divisions of Wildcats to escort SBDs and TBFs on a mission to bomb Japanese shipping in Vella Gulf, between Vella Lavella and Kolombangara Islands north of Guadalcanal. Two F4Fs had to turn back, and the remaining six split into two flights, with two aircraft climbing to provide high cover while 2Lt Jefferson DeBlanc led four on as close escort.

As the dive-bombers finished their runs and regrouped for the return flight, they came under attack from Type 0 Observation seaplanes. DeBlanc saw two "Petes," flying in trail, closing in on the SBDs. With his wingman, SSgt James Feliton, providing cover, DeBlanc attacked the trailing floatplane, coming in from the "six o'clock" position and setting it on fire. DeBlanc then went after the lead "Pete," again from behind. He saw flames trailing from his target following his first burst, after which the floatplane made a slow climbing turn to the right and then exploded.

Despite being low on fuel, DeBlanc and Feliton remained with the SBDs, fending off attacks from Zero-sens. DeBlanc claimed three of the fighters shot down before he was forced to bail out of his badly damaged fighter. Feliton also had to take to his parachute. With aid from coastwatchers and the Solomon Islands police force, both DeBlanc and Feliton returned to Guadalcanal 13 days later. For his actions, DeBlanc was awarded the Medal of Honor.

The maintenance facilities at Henderson Field were necessarily primitive, as demonstrated in this February 1943 photograph of a muddy dispersal area where F4F-4s apparently had engines changed, as propellers are missing from some aircraft. (Tony Holmes Collection)

beleaguered Japanese troops on Guadalcanal. US Marine Corps SBDs and TBMs went out to attack the "Tokyo Express" (the name given by Allied forces to IJN ships delivering personnel and supplies at night) at every opportunity, with US Marine Corps Wildcats serving as escorts.

On one of these escort missions, future ace 1Lt Michael Yunck ran into a formation of Type 0 Observation seaplanes trying to intercept US Marine Corps SBDs attacking enemy ships north of Guadalcanal. Yunck had trained as a Naval Aviator and received his commission as a second lieutenant in the US Marine Corps in September 1941. He then joined Marine Observation Squadron VMO-251 and traveled with the unit to the Pacific. Yunck was shot down in an F4F in early November, and upon his return to flying status transferred to VMF-112.

On December 3, 1942, Yunck led a division of four Wildcats escorting SBDs from VMSB-142 and TBFs from VMSB-131 on a late afternoon mission against shipping 160 miles from Guadalcanal. Reaching the enemy vessels, he and the other Wildcat pilots were flying behind and above the SBDs as they were about to start their dives when Yunck saw a formation of IJNAF biplanes approaching. Capt Nathan Post Jr, who was leading a section, identified the Japanese aircraft as E8N Type 95 Reconnaissance seaplanes, and claimed three shot down in the combat that followed. Yunck correctly identified them as F1M Type 0 Observation seaplanes, which US Marine Corps pilots at the time simply identified as float biplanes. Years later he recalled the mission in an interview:

Oh, there must have been 10, 11, 12 of them. And, boy, there they were. So they started in – the SBDs started in, started down. And we were kind of behind. And they came in and started in on the SBDs, and then we were coming in on them. And it was just one of those things where you're going to catch them – meet them at the pass, you know. And they saw us, and they broke away from the SBDs, and then they all came at us head-on. And here are these four F4Fs and these 11 or so float biplanes, and we just went like that, flew right through each other. And we really had a hassle with them. And they were really good.

They were aggressive, and I had to break away because I didn't want to die in one of these head-ons. I got into two head-ons, the first one and then a second one. And both times we pressed on in – and I don't know why in the hell I couldn't hit these guys. I was shooting all the time, and I wasn't hitting them. And both times we got right in to where I said, "Holy Christ, I'm chicken," and I pulled up and went over the top on both occasions, and I swear if I hadn't I know we would have hit.

As I went over the top, the guy in the back was sitting there. Of course, I wouldn't just go over the top. I went over the top and made a nice turn around and said a prayer for this fellow in the back with his bean-shooter who was pumping me full of holes.

I got three of them, and all in deflection shots. I didn't get a shot that wasn't just darn near full deflection. And it was just a matter of, you know, where you are.

January 27, 1943

GUADALCANAL, SOLOMON ISLANDS

1 Flying without a working radio west of Henderson Field on Guadalcanal, Capt J. Hunter Reinburg of VMF-121 turns over command of his division to his element leader, then sees a group of what he assumes are Zero-sens flying several thousand feet below his division. The aircraft are in fact Imperial Japanese Army Air Force (IJAAF) Type 1 ("Oscar") fighters from 1st and 11th Sentai.

2 Diving near vertically at an "Oscar," Reinburg opens fire in a full deflection shot just as his opponent spots the threat and tries to evade. It is too late, and the Wildcat's 0.50-cal. rounds strike the IJAAF fighter.

3 Pulling hard out of his dive, Reinburg looks back and sees the "Oscar," plunging in flames towards the jungle below.

4 Gaining level flight, Reinburg spots a second "Oscar," climbing to attack him and turns to engage it. Staying above the enemy fighter, he dives in the direction of his opponent.

5 As the "Oscar" frantically turns, Reinburg passes close to his target, the Wildcat diving and the IJAAF fighter climbing. The two aircraft then separate.

6 Reinburg looks back and spots what may be the same "Oscar" turning to re-engage him again, so he dives on the enemy fighter once more, this time catching it from directly above. Shells from his six 0.50-cal. machine guns slam into the "Oscar," which eventually explodes.

7 As Reinburg climbs back up to altitude, he spots six more "Oscars" flying in close formation near Savo Island. They do not see the lone American fighter, and he begins to stalk the rearmost "Oscar" from below.

8 Once in range, Reinburg opens fire. Only a single gun is operable, however, and the resulting recoil snap-rolls the Wildcat into a diving right-hand turn.

9 Seeing the tracer, the IJAAF pilots turn to attack Reinburg.

10 Diving at high speed toward Guadalcanal, Reinburg pulls out with only feet to spare and races back to Henderson Field, and safety.

11 Unable to catch the heavier American fighter, the "Oscar" pilots give up the chase and turn away.

Following the intense aerial battles fought over Guadalcanal during October and November, IJNAF land-based Zero-sen units continued to fly fighter sweeps from Rabaul and newly built bases on Bougainville to cover IJN vessels running supplies to Japanese troops fighting on the island. (Author's Collection)

All of a sudden, there's one there, and so you say, "oh, go after him." And then all of a sudden, "My God, there's another one there. Should I go after him?" and in the meantime, there's one coming in here, and I better get the hell out. And so it was just a real gaggle, and everybody stayed in there real close. And we know that of the 11, at least seven or eight were knocked down.

The F1M pilots in this combat claimed four American aircraft shot down and five probables, for the loss of five "Petes."

During January 1943, Zero-sens from 204th and 252nd Kokutai flew regular patrols down the "Slot" covering IJN ships carrying supplies to Guadalcanal, and toward the end of the month attempted to gain air superiority over the embattled island as the Japanese began withdrawing their remaining troops from the island. Countering these missions brought future ace Capt J. Hunter Reinburg his first claims of the war. He had been commissioned as a second lieutenant in the US Marine Corps in February 1941, and had spent most of 1942 flying defensive missions out of Samoa, before transferring to VMF-121 in December. Reinburg made his first claim – a Zero-sen – on January 15, 1943 during an action that saw US Marine Corps F4F squadrons claim 13 IJNAF fighters shot down around Vella Lavella Island.

On January 27 he was again engaged in combat with "Zero-sens" (actually Ki-43 "Oscars" from the IJAAF's 1st and 11th Sentai) over Guadalcanal, claiming two shot down. A missing radio and confusion over signals had led Reinburg to attack a flight of enemy fighters, perhaps rashly, on his own. In his rush to intercept an incoming raid, Reinburg had taken off with his division knowing that his Wildcat had no radio installed. He turned over the lead of the formation to his wingman, who led the division up to an altitude of 25,000ft and then began circling Henderson Field.

Shortly thereafter, Reinburg saw a formation of aircraft 4,000ft below him that he identified as "Zero" fighters and signaled to his wingman his intention to attack, unaware that his wingman had received instructions to remain over Henderson Field in case Japanese bombers came in after the fighters. Reinburg gave a hand signal that he was taking the lead again, and peeled off to dive down on the fighters below. He described the combat that followed in his memoir, *Combat Aerial Escapades – A pilot's log book*:

As soon as my plane was diving vertically, I sighted an enemy Zero who did not seem very far below me. I was not concerned with the fact that my steep angle of dive would cause me to rapidly go below him since he was flying level. My approach was designed exactly as we had attacked tow sleeves many times in practice. My gun sight pipper was sufficiently in front of him for a full deflection shot. I tripped the machine gun trigger when about 1,200ft above him and began pulling out of the dive in order to keep the sight on him.

At this instant, he apparently saw me because he executed a sharp climbing left turn. Recognizing his maneuver was the smartest thing he could do under the circumstances, it appeared my opponent was an experienced flyer. Fortunately for me, in my gunnery training I had become quite proficient at this overhead type of attack. In order to keep my guns on him, I was forced to roll left, which, in turn, further steepened my dive. I quit firing at him when passing close behind his tail.

My plane was still moving vertically down toward the earth and my excess speed carried me 2,000ft below the Zero before regaining level flight. Excessive G loads strained me and the airplane in the pull-out as I attempted to retain sight of my enemy. However, the pull of gravity was so great on my body that my eyes went dim because of blood being forced out of my head, and I could not keep track of my adversary.

I was sure my bullets had hit the Zero, but I went below him so quickly it was impossible to ascertain any damage. However, as full sight returned to me following a near blackout, I was happy to see his plane burning and plunging toward the Guadalcanal jungle.

Knowing there were many more enemy airplanes in the area, I let my victim fall and used my excess speed to zoom back up to higher altitudes. Upon leveling off at about 20,000ft feet on a westerly course, I spotted another Zero about 3,000ft below coming toward me.

Capt J. Hunter Reinburg, flying with VMF-121, encountered enemy fighters on two missions during January 1943 and claimed three of them shot down. Later that year, flying with F4U Corsair-equipped VMF-122 (a unit he subsequently led), Reinburg claimed two Zero-sens and two "Betty" bombers shot down to "make ace." (DM-SD-03-09978, NARA)

Instantly, it was apparent that I would have to execute another overhead pass to quickly bear my guns on him. There was no time to maneuver for an easier tail shot, and he did not appear to see me. I rolled over and dove straight for him. Just as I pressed the trigger, he performed the same evasive action as his buddy. I screwed into the same left turning dive, which again increased my dive angle and gave me less time to shoot at him. I passed quite close to him in the opposite direction, with the Jap climbing and me diving, and we separated rapidly. By the time the Cat was out of the dive and climbing again in the direction I had last seen the Jap, there was no trace of him.

Moments later, I saw another Zero, or perhaps the same one, 2,000ft below me a half-mile away and going away from me at right angles. Since my plane was already running at full throttle I took up the chase. He apparently saw me and turned to meet the challenge. Having the altitude advantage, I wanted to keep it. He was climbing almost toward me and I was trying to climb up over him, hoping to execute another of those overhead passes. When the time seemed right, I rolled over and dove at him. Realizing he might make my shot harder by continuing a left turn like his two buddies, I opened fire at 1,500ft. I was upside-down, pulling into a vertical dive some 900ft from him, which was the distance where my six 0.50-cal. machine guns converged to a point. It was the ideal distance, and I was exhilarated to see his plane explode from the concentrated bullets. An instant later, I was executing another straining pullout below the confettied enemy fighter plane.

Reinburg saw another formation of "Zero-sens" above him and tried to make one more pass, from below, but only one of his guns was working. The recoil and his slow speed in the climb put him into a snap roll and a diving right turn, which was fortunate as the enemy fighters had spotted the attack and had begun turning to follow him. Reinburg was able to dive away and return safely, only to be accused of disobeying instructions to remain over Henderson Field, which infuriated him.

In February 1943, VMF-124 brought the first F4U Corsairs to Guadalcanal. Over the next three months, US Marine Corps Wildcat squadrons converted to the more capable Chance Vought fighter, with VMF-213 converting in March, VMF-121 in April, VMF-112 and VMF-221 in May, VMF-122 and VMF-214 in June, and VMF-123 in July. The US Marine Corps Wildcat's swan song in the South Pacific appears to have taken place on April 7, 1943 during the heavy attack on Guadalcanal that was part of the Japanese Operation *I-Go* offensive.

Following setbacks in operations against Allied forces in New Guinea and the Solomons, Imperial General Headquarters in Tokyo was determined to reverse Japan's fortunes and strengthen its position in both areas. Restoring Japanese air superiority over New Guinea and the Solomons before the Allies could bring in more air power would be critical. For Operation *I-Go*, the IJNAF posted in aircraft from the Combined Fleet carriers *Zuikaku, Zuiho, Hiyo,* and *Junyo*, adding more than 180 fighters, dive- and torpedo-bombers to the three land-based air flotillas gathering at Rabaul and on Bougainville.

As a preliminary to the start of the offensive, a large force of Zero-sens carried out a fighter sweep to the Guadalcanal area on April 1 to knock

down as many American fighters as possible. VMF-221's Wildcats joined VMF-124's Corsairs intercepting the raid, and F4F pilot 1Lt William Snider claiming three Zero-sens shot down.

The attack on the afternoon of April 7 involved the largest number of Japanese aircraft ever seen in the South Pacific. Their target was American shipping around Guadalcanal, with two formations numbering 47 Zero-sens in total ranging ahead of an attacking force that comprised four separate units flying 70 "Val" dive-bombers, each with an escort of 26–30 Zero-sens. The combined force totaled 238 aircraft.

Amongst the units defending Guadalcanal were Wildcat-equipped VMF-214 and VMF-221, and they found themselves in the thick of the action. Pilots from VMF-214 claimed four "Vals" and six "Zero-sens" that afternoon for the loss of one Wildcat shot down and another that crashed on landing after being shot up by enemy fighters.

VMF-221, which had scrambled 16 Wildcats, was directed toward Tulagi to attack the approaching dive-bombers. Lt James Swett took his division down to attack the "Vals," only to quickly lose two Wildcats and eventually get shot down himself by return fire from the aircraft he was attacking. By then, however, Swett had claimed seven shot down and an eighth as a probable in an incredible feat of airmanship that resulted in him receiving a well-earned Medal of Honor.

VMF-221's remaining divisions tangled with the Zero-sens, and lost five Wildcats in a swirling combat. Two F4Fs were ditched, one pilot bailed out and two more force-landed, their Wildcats wrecked – remarkably, all five pilots survived. Most of the remaining F4Fs were damaged, some badly, but they managed to land back at "Fighter Two" on Guadalcanal, having claimed ten Zero-sens shot down.

The Wildcat continued to soldier on flying CAPs over Guadalcanal and nearby islands, and escorting the SBDs and TBFs attacking Japanese shipping and positions in the Central Solomons. Extending the fighter's already ample range when flying offensive, rather than defensive, missions meant fitting F4F-4s with underwing 58-gallon drop tanks, as seen here. (127GR-3-58842, RG127, NARA)

Future ace 2Lt Donald Balch made his first claims during this fraught mission. One of the newer pilots in VMF-221, he had received his wings in July 1942. Years later, he described this memorable mission:

We were in our ready room at "Fighter Two" on Guadalcanal when we were notified of an approaching group, consisting possibly of Japanese aircraft. We were scrambled, my entire squadron, and my division was sent to 20,000ft for the intercept. We were flying F4F-4s at the time, and it took us a while to get up there. Upon arriving at 20,000ft, we made one circle and were attacked by a group of Zeros. We all went in different directions, and I found myself on the tail of an enemy aircraft, a Zero, which I promptly shot down. I saw him go down smoking and in flames.

I then looked around for the rest of my flight, and I didn't see anybody. But as I was looking down, I spotted another Zero about 1,000ft below me at two o'clock. I nosed over and dove down on him, approaching him from the rear, and when I got within range I started shooting, but I only had two guns operating at that point. As soon as I started shooting, this aircraft pulled up and did what looked like a snap Immelmann to me. The next thing I knew, he was heading for me, practically head-on. We went by each other, and I turned around and saw him dive out toward the ocean. I then lost sight of him as I was maneuvering. I never saw him again.

This has remained in my mind since the event took place in 1943, and I have often wondered what happened to that Japanese pilot. I know I hit him, but as I

During the early months of 1943, and again in June and July of that year, the US Navy sent several Wildcat squadrons to Guadalcanal from nearby land bases and from escort carriers serving in the South Pacific. These F4F-4s of VF-27, which undertook two spells ashore in the Solomons, are preparing to take off from the flightdeck of *Suwanee* at the start of the year. (80G-470121, RG80, NARA)

say, I only had two guns operating. There were no other aircraft in sight, and so I headed back toward "Fighter Two" in Guadalcanal, where I landed and found the rest of the members of my flight had already come in.

Balch's Wildcat was one of the few that did not receive any damage from the Zero-sens during the combat.

While the US Marine Corps was rapidly converting its F4F squadrons to the F4U, the US Navy continued to employ the Wildcat in combat in the South Pacific during the first half of 1943, sending several squadrons ashore to Guadalcanal from the escort carriers then serving in the South Pacific. VGF-11 was one such unit, having flown off USS *Altamaha* (ACV-18/CVE-18) to Guadalcanal, from where its pilots claimed ten Zero-sens shot down on February 4 and 7. Redesignated VF-21 in May 1943, the squadron returned to Guadalcanal the following month.

From March 10 to April 25, 1943, VF-26 from USS *Sangamon* (CVE-26), VF-27 from USS *Suwanee* (CVE-27), and VF-28 from USS *Chenango* (CVE-28) all operated from Guadalcanal, participating in the pre-Operation *I-Go* clash on April 1 – VF-27 and VF-28 claimed nine Zero-sens shot down between them. The three squadrons returned to Guadalcanal between June 26 and August 5, where they joined VF-11, which had arrived on April 26 with 34 Wildcats. The latter unit was land-based at the time due to the lack of carriers in the Pacific Fleet. During June and July, these F4F squadrons would participate in several intense combats with Zero-sen-equipped 204th, 251st, and 582nd Kokutai based at Buka Island and Buin, on Bougainville. The US Navy Wildcat pilots would find that despite these IJNAF units having suffered heavy losses, the surviving Zero-sen pilots were still dangerous adversaries.

1025 hrs, JUNE 12, 1943

RUSSELL ISLAND, SOLOMON ISLANDS

1 Lt William Leonard is leading his division of four VF-11 F4F-4s at 26,000ft near New Georgia on a mission to protect a US Navy PBY Catalina.

2 Leonard sees 20 to 30 aircraft ahead of him, flying above and below his altitude. He identifies these as Zero-sens (from either 251st or 582nd Kokutai) and orders his division to make one pass and then break off, as they do not have enough fuel for a prolonged fight.

3 With the Zero-sens maneuvering at all levels, the engagement quickly degenerates into a free-for-all. The Wildcat pilots fight singly in the same general area, while P-40s and F4Us arrive and start engaging enemy aircraft above the Wildcats.

4 Leonard makes passes at several Zero-sens, seeing one of his targets burst into flames.

5 Losing altitude, Leonard makes several more passes, missing some Zero-sens but setting another on fire.

6 Finding himself at 16,000ft, below the combat and low on gas, Leonard breaks off and forms up with another Wildcat for the flight back to Guadalcanal.

VF-11 had been flying from Guadalcanal for nearly six weeks before the squadron made its first claims. On June 7, 1943, two separate Wildcat flights were credited with downing three Zero-sens for the loss of three F4Fs, whose pilots were saved. Five days later, the squadron had its first big day when it joined other units intercepting a fighter sweep comprising 77 Zero-sens from all three fighter Kokutai. VF-11 claimed 14 Zero-sens shot down for the loss of one Wildcat that ditched. During the fight, Lt(jg) Vernon Graham, a section leader in Lt William Leonard's division, claimed five fighters shot down in his first aerial combat, as he described in the squadron's Aircraft Action Report:

We (Leonard's division) with two other planes were in a loose formation when we moved in on the fight at 25,000ft. A Zero got on either LEONARD's or IVIE's [Lt(jg) Claude Ivie] tail and did a slow roll. I came in on him with an overhead, fired a short burst, and he broke into flames. All the F4F-4s had split up and single combats were going on all around. There were some F4Us up above.

VF-11's first ace made the grade the hard way – five victories in one mission. Lt(jg) Vernon E. Graham was engaged in the June 12, 1943 combat near the Russell Islands when, although low on fuel, Lt Bill Leonard led a pass at no fewer than 77 inbound Zero-sens. In the ensuing combat, Graham claimed four enemy fighters destroyed. As he turned to land on the emergency field on the Russell Islands, his fuel almost exhausted, he attacked another fighter tailing a Corsair. Graham took a snap shot, lost sight of the enemy, and then made a forced landing. However, he overshot the short runway and crashed into the trees. While Graham was in hospital recuperating, the F4U pilot he had saved expressed his thanks and confirmed the destruction of the fifth Zero-sen. (Tony Holmes Collection)

Suddenly, I saw a Zero on my left and a little below. I made a high-side attack and set him afire. Looking down, I saw another Zero about 150ft below coming around toward me in a climbing turn. I pulled up and the Zero rolled over on his back and pushed his stick forward to meet me head on. This maneuver put my pipper dead on him and I opened fire. He exploded. I don't think he even fired on me.

At this time Capt [Kenneth] Ford of VMF-121 came by and gave me the joining up signal. Another F4U was with us and we went over to take on four Zeros. We were scissoring on one another when one of the Marines drew a Zero on his tail right across my path and I gave him a burst. The air was filled with flying pieces of his plane when my six 0.50-cals. went in him, and some of them were so close I thought they would hit me.

By now I was close to the Russells and almost out of gas. I saw another Zero ahead and above me, so I pulled up and opened fire at about 350 yards. He began to smoke, rolled over, and headed down. I did not see what happened to him, but Capt Ford, who was with me, reported that this Zero crashed in the water. Then I ran out of gas and two Zeros jumped my tail. The Marines shot one down off my tail and chased the other one off.

I came on down to the Russells strip, and because my plane was so light, all my gas and ammunition being gone, I overran the runway and cracked up.

An IJNAF Type 99 "Val" goes down during the combat of June 16, 1943, when the Japanese launched a major raid against American shipping around Guadalcanal and Tulagi. That day, the attacking force lost 13 Type 99 Carrier Dive-Bombers to American fighters, with VF-11 being responsible for the destruction of most of them. (80G-213318, RG80, NARA)

Graham was seriously injured attempting to land his fighter on an airstrip on the Russell Islands, being rendered unconscious when he fractured his skull. It was not until he recovered consciousness in hospital, and the US Marine Corps pilots from VMF-121 had submitted their Aircraft Action Reports, that VF-11 learned what had happened during the combat. For his success on June 12, Graham received the Navy Cross. US Marine Corps and US Navy squadrons had claimed 26 Zero-sens shot down for the loss of six fighters during this action. The IJNAF, conversely, claimed 26 American fighters shot down for the loss of seven Zero-sens and six pilots.

Four days later, VF-11 enjoyed even more success when its pilots claimed 15 "Vals" and 13 Zero-sens shot down. The leading scorers were future aces Lt(jg) Charles Stimpson, who was credited with four "Vals," and Lt(jg) James Swope, who claimed three. In the hectic combat on June 16, no fewer than 104 Allied fighters had intercepted 60 "Val" dive-bombers and their 70 Zero-sen escorts, claiming 45 of the latter shot down and 32 dive-bombers for the loss of six Allied fighters. Although the IJNAF of course lost far fewer aircraft than had been claimed, the units involved were still hit hard. Some

In the combat on June 16, Lt(jg) Charles Stimpson of VF-11 claimed four "Vals" shot down for his first claims against Japanese aircraft. "Skull" Stimpson, who claimed six Japanese aircraft over the Solomons, completed a second tour with VF-11 in late 1944. Flying over the Philippines, he claimed an additional ten Japanese fighters to take his final tally to 16. (2011-06-25_ image 001_01, John W. Lambert Photograph Collection, Museum of Flight, Seattle)

13 "Vals" and ten Zero-sens had been shot down, with four more fighters having to be force-landed on their return to base.

Stimpson's Aircraft Action Report for this large-scale engagement read as follows:

As I was first to sight the bogies in our division, I led the dive to interception, followed close behind on my port side by my section leader, Swope. The planes were easily identified as Aichi 99 Jap dive-bombers. I fired one burst at one plane just entering its dive but do not believe I hit it. I swung in behind the next plane which was just entering his dive. When I closed to what I gauged was the correct range, I opened fire. I could see my tracers going into his fuselage and the inboard trailing edges of his wings were breaking off. I believe it was his left flap that flew off, and he swung off to the left, smoking badly. Swope saw him burning and heading for the water.

Just at this time I caught a glimpse of a plane blow up just off my port side and astern which turned out to be the one that Swope hit. I was traveling at an estimated 250 knots. I pulled out violently to the right and then swung back in. I saw a plane just pulling out from his dive and came in on a slight high-side with a full deflection shot. I did not notice any return fire from his rear seat. I opened

up with about a 70 mil lead and he exploded within two to three seconds. I pulled over him and headed out between Savo and Tulagi.

I then saw three Jap dive-bombers, two in quite close formation and one a little ahead. They were at approximately 1,000ft and I had plenty of speed advantage. As I was on their port side, I decided to make a run at them from the rear. Just when I was commencing my run, a P-40 approaching low from the starboard side made a pass at my target and pulled out to the left. The Jap began to smoke a little, but held formation, so I pushed over and came in at about a 45-degree angle, shot all my guns, and he burst into flames around the cowling. Then he appeared to try to ram me by pulling up sharply to the left. I pulled to the right and saw him half-roll and dive into the water.

By this time none of my guns were firing, so I charged as many as I could and tested them. One port gun fired, so I swung down to the left on the other Jap. This is the only enemy from which I noted return fire, but his tracers were going beneath my port wing. I got in as close as I could and opened fire, seeing incendiaries hitting his engine and wing root. He began to smoke as I passed under him, and by the time I was in position for a run on his port side he was smoking badly and losing altitude fast. When I was going into another run on him, I glanced over my shoulder and saw a Zero commencing a run on me.

Lt(jg) Charles Stimpson's F4F-4 BuNo 12163, showing four kill markings under the cockpit, the VF-11 squadron insignia forward of the windscreen and the name BILLSIE behind the cowling. Since they were based on land and not on a carrier, where aircraft were constantly re-spotted, VF-11 pilots could routinely fly their own individual aircraft. The fighter is also fitted with underwing 58-gallon drop tanks. (2011-06-25_image 002_01, John W. Lambert Photograph Collection, Museum of Flight, Seattle)

I threw my fighter into a violent nose dive flipper turn away from him. He hit me with about five 7.7mm rounds, and I found out later that Swope made a pass and mixed with him, which explained why I did not see him again. I was nearly out of ammunition, so I stayed low on the water and returned to base.

Two weeks later, it was VF-21's turn to be the high-scoring Wildcat squadron when it claimed 32 Japanese aircraft shot down in two missions on June 30, 1943. That morning, US Army troops landed on Rendova Island, with the aim of establishing a base there to support operations against New Georgia, due north of the island, where the Japanese had established an airfield at Munda.

Fighters turned back a morning sweep by 27 Zero-sens, some of which carried bombs. In the early afternoon, a further 24 IJNAF fighters from 251st Kokutai escorted 26 torpedo-carrying "Betty" bombers targeting shipping supporting the landing on Rendova. Forty-eight F4Us and F4Fs intercepted the enemy formation, claiming 29 bombers and 49 fighters shot down. The US Marine Corps and US Navy fighters had indeed devastated the bomber formation, downing 20 "Bettys." Only eight Zero-sens had been destroyed, however. During the day, VF-21 lost four Wildcats and two pilots in combat.

In the afternoon, the squadron sent up 28 Wildcats in two formations – one of four divisions with 15 aircraft and the other with three divisions of 13 aircraft. One formation of Wildcats was patrolling at 16,000ft west of Munda and the other formation at 7,000ft when they were alerted to incoming Japanese aircraft. Pilots soon spotted a formation of what they estimated to be 15 to 18 twin-engined bombers, and when they went after them, the Naval Aviators were quickly intercepted by defending Zero-sens. Lt(jg) William Smith and his wingman, future ace Ens Gerald Boyle, each claimed a "Betty" and two Zero-sens shot down, as they noted in the squadron's Aircraft Action Report. Smith recalled:

When I first saw the bombers they were at 4,000–5,000ft and were over the east side of Munda. We dove for the second V formation of three planes. I got the leader on the first pass. On the second pass, I made a run on the starboard wingman, but even when I left him smoking he did not break formation. At this time I saw F4Fs

This photograph was taken late in VF-11's Guadalcanal tour, and the 48 victory flags on the propeller blades suggest mid-June 1943. The middle prop blade also shows six purple hearts in testament to the casualties suffered by the unit. The 33 pilots seen here are short of VF-11's full roster, since four Naval Aviators had been evacuated due to wounds or illness. (Tony Holmes Collection)

engaged with the Zeros overhead. After my second run, I pulled up to scissor and got one Zero on a low-side run. He burst into flames. I turned and shot at another and he too burst into flames. I made a high-side approach on his starboard wing.

At this point a Zero I had not seen let go a burst, and I dove and got into cloud cover. When I came out, the fight was over and I had time to look around. I know I saw two tramp steamers smoking heavily and two other small craft, possibly LSTs. I joined up with the rest of my flight and we came home together.

I can confirm Ens Boyle's bomber, and the fact that there were at least seven burning on the water.

Boyle gave the following account of his actions during the clash with the IJNAF bombers and their fighter escort:

After the first pass at the Betty formation, which was proceeding on a course of about 250°, I saw Zeros diving in on our fighters that were attacking their bombers. We (Smith and myself) pulled up and made another pass at the bombers – both times ineffective for me, since I was not able to get into a position to get a good shot at them.

As we pulled out of the second dive, a Zero came in on Smith's quarter. I dropped back and took a shot at him to chase him off, but, when he recovered, Smith had gotten away from me. I pushed over, figuring that he had made another run at the bombers. I couldn't see him, however, and when I rolled around to see the bombers, I found I had one in my sights at a very close range. I only got in a very short burst, but I saw him break into flames across and between the engines.

I pulled out [of the attack] with a Zero on my tail. This was taken off by another F4F. As I pulled up, a Zero made a turn up and away from me, presenting a silhouette target. I fired and he rolled over and burst into flames directly behind the cockpit. Another Zero then came in on me, firing from about 50–75ft, but he left only one 7.7mm hole in my fuselage. He was taken off by two F4Fs.

Next, I turned to see a Zero on another F4F's tail – he was very close but did not seem to be firing. I started firing at him from a distance out, and I kept it up as I closed 90° from him. I saw smoke from his engine, and when he dipped his nose to dive, flames sprang up from his whole left wing.

Vega [the fighter director] then called and asked all fighters to get at the shipping, but when I got there, the bombers were nowhere in sight. A few Zeros were at about 10,000ft, but the F4Fs and F4Us were forming over the ships. When we got there the ships chased us all away with a barrage of AA.

Regular CAPs continued over Rendova and New Georgia for the rest of July. By the time VF-11 left Guadalcanal on July 12, its pilots had claimed 55 enemy aircraft destroyed for the loss of 12 Wildcats in aerial combat. VF-21 appears to have been the last F4F squadron to have claimed Japanese aircraft in the South Pacific, with seven pilots on patrol over Rendova on July 25 running into formations of attacking Zero-sens. The combat that ensued was representative of all the hard-fought battles US Marine Corps and US Navy Wildcat squadrons had experienced over the prior year against the A6M. That afternoon, VF-21 pilots claimed seven Zero-sens destroyed at a cost of three F4Fs.

AFTERMATH

The withdrawal of the US Navy's Wildcat squadrons from the South Pacific was by no means the end of the Grumman fighter's combat. The F4F belongs to a select group of American military aircraft that were in service from the beginning to the very end of the nation's participation in World War II. To make room at Grumman for production of the F6F Hellcat, the US Navy shifted production of the Wildcat, and the TBF Avenger, to the General Motors Corporation, using General Motors' automobile factories in New York, New Jersey, and Maryland. Organized into the General Motors Eastern Aircraft Division, in late 1942 these factories began building the F4F-4 as the FM-1 and the TBF-1 as the TBM-1.

While the Hellcat replaced the Wildcat on board the US Navy's large Essex-class fleet carriers and smaller Independence-class light carriers, there was a need for a fighter that could equip the many new escort carriers being built for both the US Navy and for the British Royal Navy. Initially, FM-1s flew from CVEs, but the US Navy soon asked Grumman to develop an improved version of the Wildcat specifically for the shorter flightdecks of the escort carriers.

By then Wright Aeronautical had developed a more powerful version of the Wright R-1820 Cyclone engine (fitted with forged cylinders) that proved to be lighter than the Pratt & Whitney R-1830. The Cyclone generated 1,350hp, some 150hp more than the R-1830. Grumman mated the new R-1820-56 Cyclone with the XF4F-8 airframe and, after testing, added a taller vertical tail to cope with the increased torque of the more powerful Wright engine. Grumman lightened the new fighter by removing two of the 0.50-cal. machine guns from the wings. With a more powerful engine and a lighter airframe, the XF4F-8 proved to be slightly faster than the F4F-4, but with a substantially better rate of climb that was almost double that of the earlier Wildcat and a shorter take-off distance – both critical for service from smaller escort carriers.

The new fighter went into production at the General Motors Eastern Aircraft Division in 1943 as the FM-2. By the time the final example had

The FM-2 was the final, and much improved, version of the Wildcat, being lighter and fitted with a more powerful Wright R-1830-56 engine giving 1,350hp. The FM-2 gave excellent service on US Navy escort carriers, with this example seen launching from USS *Core* (CVE-13) in the North Atlantic on April 12, 1944. (National Museum of Naval Aviation)

been completed, the Eastern Aircraft Division had built 4,437 for the US Navy and an additional 340 for the Fleet Air Arm as the Wildcat VI.

The FM-2 could carry drop tanks or bombs, and later versions featured fittings for six 5-in. High Velocity Aircraft Rockets. The escort carriers in the Pacific usually embarked one composite squadron (VC) with a mix of FM-1/2 and TBM aircraft. The FM versions of the Wildcat provided close air support to landings across the Pacific, notably during the invasion of the Philippines and Okinawa. During the war, FM-1/2 pilots achieved an astonishing ratio of 32.5 Japanese aircraft destroyed for each FM lost in aerial combat. Admittedly, most victories claimed in the final Pacific campaigns consisted of more obsolete Japanese aircraft flown by poorly trained pilots.

SELECTED SOURCES

Bergerud, Eric M., *Fire in the Sky – The Air War in the South Pacific* (Westview Press, Boulder, Colorado, 2000)

Carl, Maj Gen Marion E., with Barrett Tillman, *Pushing the Envelope – The Career of Fighter Ace and Test Pilot Marion Carl* (Naval Institute Press, Annapolis, Maryland, 1994)

DeBlanc, Jefferson J., *The Guadalcanal Air War – Col. Jefferson DeBlanc's Story* (Pelican Publishing Company, Gretna, Louisiana, 2008)

Foss, Joe, with Donna Wild Foss, *A Proud American – The Autobiography of Joe Foss* (Pocket Books, New York, New York, 1992)

Lundstrom, John B., *The First Team and the Guadalcanal Campaign – Naval Fighter Combat from August to November 1942* (Naval Institute Press, Annapolis, Maryland, 1994)

Mersky, Peter B., *Whitey – The Story of Rear Admiral E. L. Feightner, A Navy Fighter Ace* (Naval Institute Press, Annapolis, Maryland, 2014)

Miller, Thomas G., Jr, *The Cactus Air Force – The Story of the Handful of Fliers who Saved Guadalcanal* (Harper & Row, Publishers, New York, New York, 1969)

Prados, John, *Islands of Destiny – The Solomons Campaign and the Eclipse of the Rising Sun* (New American Library, New York, New York, 2012)

Reinburg, J. Hunter, *Aerial Combat Escapades – A Pilot's Log Book* (Carlton Press, New York, New York, 1966)

Reynolds, Clark G., *The Saga of Smokey Stover – From His Diary* (Tradd Street Press, Charleston, South Carolina, 1978)

Sherrod, Robert, *History of Marine Corps Aviation in World War II* (Combat Forces Press, Washington, D.C., 1952)

Tillman, Barrett, *The Wildcat in World War II* (Nautical & Aviation Publishing Company of America, Annapolis, Maryland, 1983)

Tillman, Barrett, *Osprey Aircraft of the Aces 3 – Wildcat Aces of World War 2* (Osprey Publishing, London, 1995)

Young, Edward M., *Osprey Duel 54 – F4F Wildcat vs A6M Zero-sen – Pacific Theater 1942* (Osprey Publishing, Oxford, 2013)

INDEX

Note: references to images are in **bold**.